LIGHTS-OUT PUTTING

LIGHTS-OUT PUTTING

A Mind, Body, and Soul Approach to Golf's Game Within the Game

TODD SONES

PGA Professional, ranked as one of the top 100 teaching professionals in America by *Golf Magazine*

with David DeNunzio

A MOUNTAIN LION BOOK

CONTEMPORARY BOOKS

Library of Congress Cataloging-in-Publication Data

Sones, Todd.
    Lights-out putting: a mind, body, and soul approach to golf's game within the game / Todd Sones with David DeNunzio.
      p.   cm.
    ISBN 0-8092-2440-2
    1. Putting (Golf).   I. Title.
GV979.P8 565   2000
796.352/35 21   00-21799
                                                  CIP

Jacket design by Amy Yu Ng
Jacket photograph copyright © Wayne Chasan/The Image Bank
Interior design by Hespenheide Design
Interior photographs on pages 7, 11, 51, 65, 86, 106, 115, and 137 by Steve Werner.
All other interior photographs taken at Industry Hills Golf Club, City of Industry, Calif., by Warren Keating

Published by Contemporary Books
A division of NTC/Contemporary Publishing Group, Inc.
4255 West Touhy Avenue, Lincolnwood (Chicago), Illinois 60712-1975 U.S.A.
Printed in the United States of America
International Standard Book Number: 0-8092-2440-2

00 01 02 03 04 05 LB 18 17 16 15 14 13 12 11 10 9 8 7 6 5 4 3 2

Contents

Putting—Golf's Great Equalizer

Love and putting are mysteries for the philosopher to solve.
Both subjects are beyond golfers.
—**Tommy Armour**

After serious study and consideration of the many golf books on the market today, I thought it was time to write a book that provided golfers with a comprehensive look at golf's game within a game: putting. Why would I want to do such a thing? Because it's staggering how many shots players can save during a round with the putter, especially on days when the tee-to-green game isn't quite up to par. When you think back to your best rounds, I'm sure you can recall some great drives or a couple of approach shots that finished close to the pin. But overall, it was likely your putting that fueled your success. On some days, putting seems easy; you make everything you look at. Unfortunately, for most amateurs, those days are few and far between. But there's no reason why it has to be that way.

In golf, there are many things you need to do well in order to post a respectable score—for instance, drive the ball in the fairway, control the distance of your short irons and wedges, and escape greenside rough and bunkers without fear. Some players, especially those with higher aspirations, will ultimately need to develop the skills to curve the ball on command, perfect the knock-down shot and high lob, and build the confidence necessary to lace a 2-iron pin-high when the match is on the line. Regardless of a player's goals, self-discipline will always be a must; likewise for creativity, a good attitude, and, above all, a love and respect for the game.

Obviously, if you're reading this book, your goal is to become a better golfer. And it's likely that over the past weeks, months, years, or even decades, you've dedicated some of your valuable free time to perfecting the above-mentioned requirements, all with the single-minded purpose of shooting lower scores and having more fun on the course. But the fact that you've chosen a book geared solely to the art of putting tells a different story. Actually, it tells two. Story One: You understand how important putting is to your overall game. Story Two: It might be on the greens where your game needs the most improvement. If that's the case, don't be discouraged. Despite its simplicity and humble exterior, putting, for some, can be the most difficult aspect of the game to perfect.

As you'll soon discover, putting requires patience, sound fundamentals, confidence, focus, and, most important, precision. On any given putt, there's usually only a small margin for error. This fact can make even the most accomplished players tremble in their spikes. Why? Well, think of it this way: If you miss a green with a mid-iron or slice your drive into the rough, you can scramble and still salvage par. Miss a putt, on the other hand, and the stroke is gone forever.

I can't stress enough the importance of putting. That's why I'm amazed how players can spend two hours banging their drivers on the practice tee, or spend their entire preround practice time warming up their full swings, and not roll a single putt on the practice green. What these players don't realize is that you can hit every fairway and every green, but if you never make a putt, the best you can do is shoot par. Now, par is a fine score, but when was the last time you hit every fairway or every green? For most players, the answer is never. Even the best drivers in the world will miss an average of three to four fairways every round. The reason why Tour players can shoot such low scores is that they can complete a round needing only 24 to 26 putts.

Putting is golf's great equalizer. If all that mattered in golf was distance and accuracy off the tee, guys like John Daly (a big hitter) and Fred Funk (an accurate driver) would win every event on the Tour. A hot putter can propel even the shortest driver in the field—or the most erratic—to the top of the leaderboard. Nowhere is this fact clearer than in professional golf's four majors, where the best putter in the tournament is usually the player hoisting the trophy on Sunday.

The following table lists the 1999 major winners and some key statistics. Notice their Total Putts ranking versus their Average Drive ranking for each tournament. You don't need a Ph.D. to understand that putting is key to success.

TOURNAMENT	WINNER	TOTAL PUTTS (RANK)	DRIVING DISTANCE AVERAGE (RANK)
U.S. Open	Payne Stewart	111 putts (8)	255 yards (50)
U.S. Women's Open	Juli Inkster	111 (4)	246 (11)
U.S. Senior Open	Dave Eichelberger	111 (3)	272 (30)
Masters	Jose Maria Olazabal	109 (7)	240 (55)
The Tradition	Graham Marsh	52 (5)*	272 (22)
du Maurier	Karrie Webb	124 (41)	260 (7)
British Open	Paul Lawrie	112 (13)	227 (69)
Senior Players Championship	Hale Irwin	106 (1)	263 (30)
Nabisco Dinah Shore	Dottie Pepper	104 (1)	222 (71)
PGA Championship	Tiger Woods	115 (28)	308 (1)
PGA Seniors' Championship	Allen Doyle	105 (1)	250 (32)
LPGA Championship	Juli Inkster	106 (1)	282 (1)
Winner Average		**110.6 (9.4)**	**258 (31.5)**

*Final two rounds canceled due to weather

The putting-performance relationship holds true for the amateur ranks, as well, with one exception: It's more severe. Believe it or not, an improved putting technique will do more to lower your average score than better contact with your irons or a brand-new driver. The full swing is a complicated athletic movement: A minor change can take months to perfect. It's a hard fact of life that tee-to-green improvement doesn't happen overnight. I teach beginners, scratch golfers, serious junior players, college athletes, and Tour pros. When I see improvement in their scores, it most often comes from better putting than from better driving. Sure, over time, understanding and grooving a fundamentally sound full swing will elevate your game. But for near-term, tangible success, the key will always be better putting.

Take PGA Tour player Scott McCarron at the 1999 Air Canada Open, for example. McCarron made an eye-opening move from fortieth to fourth place with a sterling final-round 61. After the tournament, he said he had played just as well from tee to green on the previous day, but carded a 72. The only difference, he said, was that the majority of his putts started dropping on Sunday.

What makes a golfer a great putter? It's a combination of many factors. It begins, as all things do, with a great attitude—a belief you can make the putt. This belief results from a fundamentally sound setup, a solid stroke, the right equipment, accurate analysis of the line, and, of course, lots of practice. Golf isn't like riding a bike. Sustained improvement requires sustained practice. Unfortunately, most recreational players don't have the time or resources to do so, which may be the reason why the average handicap of American golfers hasn't changed significantly in decades.

The good news is that lower scores are attainable. With the help of this book, you'll learn the necessary steps to becoming a lights-out putter. It will provide you with knowledge and direction. The instruction on the following pages is what I use not only with amateur students, but with Tour players, as well. It's instruction that's proven to induce the most significant improvement in golfers' scores. You'll learn not only the proper putting fundamentals, but also how to put them to use each time you address a putt. You'll soon be able to effectively read the speed, slope, and grain on different greens and on every kind of putt. Imagery and confidence tools will also be presented, as will the steps involved in finding the putter that best fits your setup and stroke.

You *can* become a better putter. The ability to putt well isn't genetic. It can be learned. The first step is choosing to do so. So let's get that putter warmed up and watch those barriers start to fall!

LIGHTS-OUT PUTTING

1

Attitude Is Everything

Of all the hazards in golf, fear is the worst.
—*Sam Snead*

Of the players you know who are good to great putters, what's the single greatest contributor to their success? Is it their technique? Their commitment to practice? Their athletic skill? Their innate sense of touch? Their ability to judge slope and speed? Or is it their equipment? Likely, it's a combination of all these factors. Each is a crucial ingredient to enjoying success on the greens.

In my opinion, putting success boils down to two requirements. One, you must develop and master a sound, repeatable stroke. Two, you need a great putting attitude.

Now, don't confuse a "great" attitude with a "positive" attitude. A positive attitude will help you have more fun on the course. Fine. A great attitude will help you become deadly on the greens.

Traits of a Great Putting Attitude

A great putting attitude starts with thinking that you're a great putter. This belief is fueled by the development of advanced mental skills, as well as the trust you place in them. It's heightened by your reliance on feel rather than mechanics, and is maintained by confidence—a mental state that begins and ends with knowing how to get the ball into the hole.

This chapter focuses on the mind-set and personality of a great putter—a lights-out putter. Throughout the next several pages, we'll go over ways to construct such a mental outlook when faced with putts of all lengths, speeds, and breaks. But before we dive into these exercises, we have to get a grip on what exactly we're trying to develop. Outlined below are the eight must-have mental skills of a great putter, or, as I like to refer to them, "The Great Eight."

Greatness

Great putters possess a unique mind-set, one that separates them from average and/or good putters. How does this attitude differ? Well, for starters, great putters believe they're great. They're cocky—and I mean that with the greatest respect. Average or poor putters don't view themselves as great. They view themselves as average or poor putters.

The reason why most amateurs have such low putting self-esteem is that they focus solely on the putts they miss during a typical round. It's impossible to build yourself up if you look only at your mistakes. You must learn to shift your focus—and memory—toward the many putts you make, not the ones that lip out or go screaming past the hole.

Great putters, in addition to believing they're great, enjoy the task of putting. Very rarely do the words "enjoy" and "putting" find their way into the same sentence, especially if you're talking about tame, little three- and four-footers. But putting can be a thrill, especially when the match is on the line or when the leaders make their way down the homestretch during a final round on the Tour. Believing that holing a putt is just as rewarding as nailing a 275-yard drive right down the heart of the fairway is a major step toward developing a great putting attitude.

When one of my students says they find putting enjoyable, they're also telling me they're up to the many challenges of rolling the ball into the hole. They're not concerned about missing—or the tricky putt they'll have coming back if they do indeed miss the cup. This thought process is in contrast to the mental outlook of average putters, who dread long, breaking putts and must-make four-footers. Make no mistake, great putters "love" to putt.

There's a great story about Gary Player, who, during the Tour's Florida swing, often said how he loved to putt on the slow, grainy greens of the South. When the Tour ventured north, Player would change gears and rank slick, bent-grass greens as the best surfaces to putt on. When confronted with the fact that he couldn't possibly love both extremes, Player simply responded that he loved to putt on all greens, "especially those I have to play on today."

Confidence

Over the years I've had the privilege to work with Dr. Glenn Albaugh, a performance specialist who trains Scott McCarron, among numerous professional clients. Glenn has had a great deal of influence on my teaching philosophies. One of the many

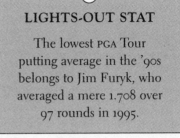

LIGHTS-OUT STAT

The lowest PGA Tour putting average in the '90s belongs to Jim Furyk, who averaged a mere 1.708 over 97 rounds in 1995.

things he's taught me is there are two types of confidence, external confidence and internal confidence. Both are required in order to develop a great putting attitude. External confidence is based on events you can't always control. It happens solely when you make putts. The problem with external confidence is that it disappears as soon as you miss a few easy putts. When it's gone, it's hard to recover. Players who possess only external confidence continually alter their strokes, setups, or equipment in a desperate attempt to find that mythical magic bullet.

Great putters possess internal confidence. Internal confidence is learned and developed from the inside. It can't be taken from you if you miss putts or have a bad day. It's a deep-seated belief, based on consistent, positive self-talk, a trust in your setup, stroke, and equipment, as well as your knowledge of the greens.

Players who possess internal confidence never make wholesale changes in their mechanics, or panic when their strokes go a little haywire. And rarely do they change their equipment. The only times you should consider buying a new putter are when your putter fails to match your setup and stroke, or when new technology mandates improved results. Remember, some of the greatest putters in the history of the game used the same putter model for their entire career.

Decisiveness

A lights-out putter is a decisive putter. A player who continually changes his or her mind on the putting surface is prone to doubt. Being decisive means making decisions and putting those decisions into action without hesitation. Great putters are very resolute. They develop a detailed and exact plan on how to sink their putts. They read the break, gauge the speed, then choose a line—and remain committed to that decision.

An average putter will doubt his or her decisions and change his or her mind often. A doubter has a hard time making a good stroke, because he or she hasn't decided how the ball will react once contact is made. It's hard to hit a solid putt without a clear idea of what you're trying to do. That's what makes the science of green reading (as we'll see in Chapter 6) such an important skill to perfect. If you can accurately gauge the slope, grain, and speed, you'll free your mind of doubt and turn your focus solely to the task at hand: making the putt.

Imagination

Great putters use their imaginations on the green. By imagination, I mean "seeing" the ball rolling toward the target even before the putter is put into motion. Most players get too caught up with mechanics during the time they should be seeing, feeling, and trusting. If you're guilty of trying to perfect your stroke on the course, you most likely fall into this category. If you have a mechanical flaw, you need to improve your mechanics. But leave that kind of work for the practice green. A player who worries about mechanics on the course is practicing instead of playing golf.

In the end, you won't need perfect mechanics to putt well. Great putters aren't technique-oriented—they don't putt mechanically. They rely on touch and feel. They learn to get the ball into the hole without

Finding Fault

I'm sure you've fallen into the habit of working on your stroke during a round. Maybe you missed a few key putts in succession. So you find an isolated corner of the green and take a few practice strokes while your foursome finishes the hole. That's the hallmark of a mechanical putter, and it has no business in the world of lights-out putting. You may see a Tour pro make a few practice strokes after missing a putt. But usually, these players aren't practicing their strokes. They're verifying if they chose the right line, or if they allowed for enough break, and so on. They do this only because they expect to make all of their putts. When they miss, they search for clues, but rarely in their strokes.

thinking about "how" to get the ball into the hole. They've already established the "how" on the practice green. Great putters understand their methods and have faith that they work.

Responsibility and Awareness

What or who is responsible for a missed putt? Great putters don't get frustrated when they miss a putt. They realize it's not humanly possible to make every single one. Often a good putter blames a missed putt on an imperfection in the green, a spike mark, a poorly cut hole, or a misread. When you're putting well and you miss one that you expected to make, it's okay to blame something other than yourself in order to deal with the emotion. However, if you're having a bad day on the greens, you may want to become more aware of the source of your misses. In other words, know your tendencies.

In a recent interview, Tiger Woods stated that he normally traces his putting problems to two errors in his setup: incorrect posture and incorrect eye alignment. If you're consistently missing putts, take responsibility. Become aware of why you missed the putt. Learn to describe your putts rather than judge them. For instance, if you miss a putt to the right, assess whether you misread the break, misjudged the speed, set up incorrectly, lost commitment to the line, or, most important, didn't trust your stroke. There's no need to become negative in your assessment. Just make the adjustment and move on.

Fear

One of the strongest emotions in golf is fear. Fear comes in many forms, such as the fear of failure, fear of embarrassment, or just the fear of missing a putt you should make. The best players in the world feel fear. It's an inescapable emotion for humans. The critical difference is in how a player responds to it. If it controls you, you're done.

The one positive aspect of fear is that it's an emotion. Having fear simply means you want to succeed and avoid failure, which is perfectly okay in my book. If you have fear, you need to become aware of where it originates and deal with it at that level. Replace it with positive emotion. Look at fear as an emotion that, if not controlled, has the potential to distract you from putting your best.

Later in this book, we'll go over the preputt routine. The preputt routine is the number-one fear buster. Instead of allowing your fears to distract you, distract your fears by getting totally involved with making your next putt. Distracting yourself out of fear is one of the goals of the preputt routine.

Effort

Most players think that the harder they try to make a putt, the better their results will be. This isn't always the case. In fact, if you over-analyze your read or anguish over your stroke, you'll fall prey to doubt. Trying too hard can cause you to focus too much of your attention on individual aspects of putting, rather than on the overall job of getting the ball into the hole. In doing so, you'll destroy your ability to putt the ball smoothly and effortlessly, resulting in a loss of feel.

Great putters know how to give their best effort, not the most effort. They don't tie themselves in knots by overanalyzing or trying too hard. Great putters allow experience and instinct to take over. They know how to get into their routine and focus. A good putter trusts more than he or she tries.

Perfection

Ben Hogan, who came as close to perfection as anyone who ever played the game, used to dream about the perfect round. He'd ace every hole, except number 18, where the ball lipped out ("I was mad as hell").

Great putters accept that they'll have good days and bad days. They understand the fact that they're human and that they can't putt well every day. If they putt poorly one day, they know they come back the next. Poor putters get upset with themselves and berate their putting ability when they miss. Remember, negative reactions reinforce the notion of being a poor putter, which explains how a bad day often becomes a prolonged slump.

Developing a Great Attitude

By now, you should know the difference between the right putting atti-tude and the wrong putting attitude. The challenge is developing one. I don't pretend to have a foolproof attitude-enhancement routine, but one thing is certain: To build up a great putting attitude, you need to adopt a plan that begins by thinking you can make every putt. It's important to recognize, however, that if you haven't been successful on the greens, a "make everything" attitude is probably not very realistic.

HALE IRWIN—A LIGHTS-OUT PUTTER

There are several golfers with four U.S. Open titles, and even a greater number with two, but only Hale Irwin has three. Since turning professional in 1976, Irwin has established himself as one of the all-time greats, and has garnered a reputation as a fantastic putter, a talent that helped him make the cut in his first 86 tournaments. And he has shown no signs of slowing down: Irwin led the Senior PGA tour in putting in 1997 and 1998.

Irwin's success stems in part from his practice. An accomplished "range rat," Irwin devotes plenty of practice time to fine-tuning his stroke—and his confidence. Irwin typically starts his putting practice by holing a three-footer, then a five-footer, then a seven-footer. In doing so, he builds a pattern of success for different stroke lengths. "My aim is to instill a positive feeling, so I get the same positive feeling standing over a 30-footer as I would standing over a three-footer."

Aside from his accomplishments and dedication to positive practice, Hale Irwin is responsible for one of the greatest putts in the history of major championship golf, on the 72nd hole of regulation in the 1990 U.S. Open at Medinah Country Club. After making birdie putts on Nos. 11, 12, 13, and 14, Irwin came to the 18th hole just two strokes behind the leader, Mike Donald, who was playing in the final group of the day. There, Irwin faced a 45-foot putt with some seven feet of right-to-left break, and a large hump between his ball and the hole. Of course, he drained the bomb and posted an early score of 280 that got him into a playoff, which he eventually won to claim his third U.S. Open title.

Start developing your attitude by making short putts. If you need to start at two feet, then start at two feet. Build to three feet, then four, and so on. During your practice, make 30 to 50 short putts in a row at least twice a week. By starting with mastering short putts, you'll begin building an inventory of positive images.

Adopting a mind-set that says "I can make everything" is the fast track toward developing a positive attitude about putting. Start today. Right now. Give yourself the privilege to build a healthy attitude about your putting. Use confident, positive words that accentuate your strengths. Tell yourself that today you've decided to become the best putter you can possibly be. Remember, all great putters constantly remind themselves that they can putt, even when the putts don't fall. Brad Faxon, one of the most consistent putters on the Tour, admits that he spends more time thinking he's a great putter than actually practicing his stroke.

I CAN MAKE EVERYTHING
*"The last thing that I let go through my mind is that I've made
a whole bunch of putts, both in practice and in play.
I've done it before, so I can do it again."*
—Justin Leonard

A technique I've learned from watching Glenn Albaugh teach is the use of action phrases. Action phrases are not to be confused with conscious swing thoughts or keys for swing mechanics. They're words or phrases that promote positive feelings. These words or phrases are usually linked back to times of peak performance. Examine the list of phrases below to see if some may provoke a positive association to a time when you putted well. If they don't bring to mind any positive associations, become aware of what words you find yourself using when you're putting well. After developing your list, learn to use them consistently.

- Let it go
- Trust
- Believe
- See
- Smooth
- Target
- Breakpoint

- Feel it
- Aim
- Tempo
- Rhythm

Confidence: The Heart of a Great Putting Attitude

Establishing a great putting attitude is one thing, but maintaining one is of equal importance. You need to develop confidence, specifically inner confidence. Inner confidence can't be taken away by a few missed putts or even a bad day. Internal confidence fuels the right putting attitude—you can't have one without the other.

The key is to understand that the foundation of putting confidence is putting competence. Confidence follows competence. This means you should practice your putting with the intent to master the skills that lead to competence. In addition to practice, there are other steps that provide a base of support for developing putting confidence. They are as follows:

Make the Choice

It's 100 percent your choice as to whether or not you want to become confident in your putting. I ask each of my students to take responsibility for how they deal with the thoughts that come into their minds. It's always the player's choice as to how they react to any situation on the golf course. Many golfers make the mistake of waiting for putts to fall before they allow themselves to feel confident. Players who react solely to outcomes rely too much on external confidence. They're controlled by what's happening around them. Strive for inner confidence. Make the choice to be confident, whether you make a dozen putts in a row or miss a couple of easy tap-ins back-to-back. Allow your confidence to come from within. That way, it will always be there.

Become Aware

Once you've made the choice to be confident, the next step is to become aware of your thoughts. During your next round, rate your focus level. Ask yourself, "Am I in tune with the present, and focused on the shot at hand?" "Is my mind drifting toward a past shot or a future hole?" "Am I preoccupied with business or family matters?" In preparing to make your next putt, you need to be totally focused on that putt.

The vehicle as to how well you do that is your preputt routine. Your preputt routine should lock your mind into the cues that allow you to focus on execution and nothing else (refer to Chapter 3 on preputt routines). Your routine is especially important when you feel the pressure of a must-make putt. Your routine should help you remain focused on the task, believe in your method, and trust your decisions, which lead to a smooth and rhythmic stroke. A routine helps you positively concentrate on your task, no matter what the situation may be. It provides many players with a sense of comfort and trust in their ability, which makes them more self-confident.

BE ROUTINE

"The key for me is to stick with the same routine. If suddenly
I've got a putt I think I have to make, and I try too hard,
I've made the situation a lot more difficult than it really is.
I think back to the last putt I've made, and retrace
the steps that prompted that success."
—Davis Love III

Trust

Great players always struggle with knowing when it's time to trust their fundamentals versus when it's time to develop or adjust their fundamentals. Can you trust something that isn't trustworthy? Every player has to answer that question for him- or herself. If you feel your setup and stroke fundamentals are sound, then your efforts to improve will be based on attitude, practice, and possibly learning or improving your green-reading skills. If you feel your stroke isn't worthy of your trust, your goal should be to gain knowledge of the setup and stroke adjustments that need to be made in order to develop fundamentals you can believe in and can count on.

Believe

Once players develop a solid stroke, they must have an unwavering belief that their method is correct. Players often have sound fundamentals, but begin changing them in the middle of the round in reaction to a few missed putts. Never make wholesale changes to your method during a round. As the old saying goes, "Dance with who you brought to the party."

Compete

Another foundation for putting competence comes from playing "under the gun" in a competitive golf tournament. Nothing can provide you with a bigger boost of confidence than sinking an important putt during a club championship or going after your best round ever. For players with seriously low putting confidence, golf tournaments become golf "tourniquets," and their putting becomes a bloodletting of serious proportions.

Many amateur players exaggerate their poor putting in past rounds and let one bad putting round affect their confidence. This is an error in attitude. What happened in the past can only hurt you when you focus on it during the present. Refocus on the present putt, and keep your attention on what you want to happen versus what you fear may happen. Use your experience and previous successes, no matter how big or small, to build the foundation for your present putting confidence. Keep in mind that all it takes is one important putt to spark renewed trust and confidence.

Finding the right putter is crucial. You need to build trust in your equipment, and treat it as if it were magic. Give your putter a name, as the great putters do. Arnold Palmer dubbed his Wilson 8802 "Old Faithful."

Practice

Practice is vital to the development of confidence. You must learn to practice with a purpose. Practice to establish feel and touch to match the speed of the greens. Practice to master the fundamentals and to groove a stroke that gives you consistent contact. Practice to develop distance control. Practice to visualize the way putts break on different slopes. Whatever your purpose, ultimately you need to establish a level of competence in your mental and physical skills that promotes self-confidence on the course.

Warm Up

A practice routine before play helps players gain confidence. Do you step out of the car and walk to the first tee without even testing the speed of the greens? As you'll read in Chapter 5, a warm-up is an excellent time to develop feel. It's a tune-up for that day's round. Remember, it's not a competition. Good players use warm-ups only to get a feeling of the ball impacting the putterhead and how well the ball is rolling.

As part of your preround warm-up, you should make at least a few short putts in a row. This should help you gain confidence by seeing, hearing, and feeling putts fall before going to the first tee. It will provide you with a recent "look" of putting success, a process to instill confidence for that day's play. Take advantage of the opportunity the warm-up provides.

Commit

Confidence comes from trusting your skill as a putter. Confidence flows from being clear in your mind about what you want to do and committing yourself to that plan. Great putters prepare themselves mentally and physically for every putt. They know the importance of staying committed to their plan. They believe they've prepared for putting success. Jack Nicklaus, Ben Crenshaw, and Gary Player all talk of the importance of being totally committed to their intended purpose or goal. That purpose is to get the ball into the hole as efficiently as possible.

Players who haven't developed confidence don't always give 100 percent to each putt. Mentally, they're giving themselves an excuse if they happen to miss. Just a hint of self-doubt opens the door for indecision on the green. And indecision is your worst enemy in putting. You must remain committed to the chosen line, to your preputt routine, to your stroke, and to the belief that you're on the way to becoming a better putter.

Use Your Imagination

Imagine success. Before you putt, see yourself setting up and stroking the putt. Visualize the ball rolling on the line you've chosen until it

Visualizing Success

Putting confidence is best built up by visualizing success. That's why it's so important to hole as many putts as you can—even if they're only two-footers—when you practice and especially when you warm up before your round. The image of the ball rolling into the hole helps your mind find a "comfort zone," a mental state that tells your body to putt without fear.

A key part of your preround warm-up should be to find this comfort zone, to develop a peaceful mind-set that you can re-create when you're out on the course. Much has been written about imagery techniques, such as picturing the ball slowly rolling toward the cup and dropping in. These techniques do work. The mind is certainly a powerful tool. But I'd rather have you develop a positive mind-set and increased confidence while actually making your stroke. Here's a compromise:

Practice putting to no target. Find an isolated area of the putting green and simply stroke putts. Putt to nowhere. Focus solely on solid contact and making a smooth, rhythmic stroke. As you perform this drill, you'll find that your body is relaxed and your stroke is smooth and flowing. More important, your mind will find its comfort zone because, without a target, there's no penalty for missing. It's a way of visualizing success without having it. Work this drill into your preround routine and your practice of those confidence-building two-footers. The experience combines the reality of putting with positive imagination.

reaches its destination: the hole. Developing such positive imagery will go a long way in helping you feel confident and comfortable just before you actually stroke your putt. The image of the ball rolling into the hole helps your mind find the "comfort zone," a mental state that allows you to putt without fear. Developing imagery skills is like most golf-related skills—it takes practice. As a part of your preputt routine, stake out a plan that develops these skills.

Engage in Self-Talk

Self-talk is something we can control but often don't. If you can control the way you talk to other people, you can control the way you talk to yourself. Learn to be your own best friend. When your best friend misses an important putt, encourage him or her, lift him or her up and try to help. Do the same thing for yourself. Berating yourself won't do anything except destroy the confidence you've worked so hard to develop.

Final Thoughts

The most important thing to remember about attitude and confidence is that it's your choice. The primary requirement of being confident is simply choosing to do so. After that, stay committed to your choice. It will take time and effort to develop the necessary mental skills to become a lights-out putter, but it will be worth it.

2

Setting Up for Putting Success

If you don't set up correctly, it's impossible
to improve. Impossible.
—**Deane Beman**

There are many ways to describe the putting stroke. I like to think of it as a series of chain reactions. Why? Because each element of the putting stroke is only as good as the elements that came before it. Which is why your setup—the starting point for every stroke you make—must be without fault. Otherwise, you'll put into motion an unending chain of mistakes, a reaction that can only be offset by consistency-robbing compensations.

In analyzing the proper setup for the putting stroke, you'll find many similarities to the setup most instructors teach for the full swing, which is somewhat of a bonus since improvements in your putting setup will benefit your game when it comes to setting up to hit your driver or irons. Yet there are certain requirements of a proper putting setup that are unique for the demands of rolling the ball into the hole on a consistent basis. They are as follows:

- Taking the proper grip
- Positioning the eyes over the golf ball
- Creating perfect posture
- Allowing the arms to hang correctly
- Establishing a balanced weight distribution

Perfecting these setup requirements will go a long way toward improving your performance on the green, as long as you focus on all of them. You won't realize any success if only your grip, aim, and stance are correct. You need all five in order to give yourself a realistic chance of making a given putt.

Taking the Proper Grip

A common theme you'll come across in this book is individuality. Golf is a very specific game in regard to the person holding the club. Short players will swing the club differently than taller ones, as will stronger players from those with less strength.

DAVID DUVAL—A LIGHTS-OUT PUTTER

On the 72nd hole of the 1999 Bob Hope Chrysler Classic, David Duval came to the tee needing an eagle three to overcome a seven-stroke deficit to both win the tournament and become only the third person in PGA Tour history to shoot 59. After a brilliant 218-yard 5-iron second shot, Duval was left with a six-footer for eagle and a place in the record books. When he coolly struck his putt, only his 23rd of the day, and it found the bottom of the cup, Duval defined himself not only as one of the world's greatest players, but as a great pressure putter.

Duval's technique, which can be applied by golfers of any level, is simple but effective because it helps relieve tension. Duval's secret is maintaining an extremely light grip pressure, so light in fact that often it looks as though the putter might fall out of his hands. The lack of tension in Duval's hands and shoulders not only helps keep him loose but creates more sensitivity and feel, which allows him to keep the putterface square to the hole for a longer period of time.

The putting grip best represents golf's individualistic nature. On the Tour, if there are 160 players playing in a given tournament, you'll find no fewer than 160 different putting grips. The strokes and hand positions may appear similar, but if you were to dissect each one, you'd discover that each is unique and honed over years of practice and experimentation.

So loosen up. Relax. Place your hands on the putter's handle in the manner in which you're the most comfortable. Go left-hand low, overlapping, split-hand—whatever provides you with the most feel and control of the putterhead. All I ask is that, when placing your hands on the club, grab as much of the grip in your palms as you possibly can. Gripping the putter with the palms, rather than the fingers, is paramount for success. If you grip a club mostly with your fingers, you'll give your wrists too much freedom to hinge and unhinge. This is ideal for the full swing, where the cocking and uncocking of the wrists work to generate power and as much clubhead speed as possible. In putting, power and excessive speed don't exist. Control and consistency are the keys. Gripping the club in your palms effectively takes your wrists out of play. As a result, your putterface will tend to stay on-line and contact the ball consistently in the sweet spot.

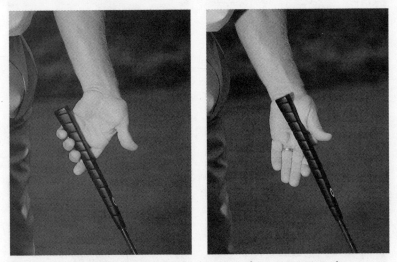

A key to consistent putting is control. If you grip the putter in your fingers, you'll give your wrists too much freedom to hinge and unhinge. For more control, place as much of the putter's grip in your palms.

If your current grip places too much of the handle in your fingers, you'll need to adjust it so more of the grip fits in your palms. The new feel may take some getting used to, but I recommend you make the change. After a few putting practice sessions, you'll begin to feel the same comfort of your old finger grip. The purpose of the grip is comfort. Holding the putter isn't an exact science. Simply get comfortable, with the single requirement of the palms playing a predominant role.

Many of my students ask what's the best putting grip. Again, the answer boils down to comfort. No less than 10 years ago, the conven-

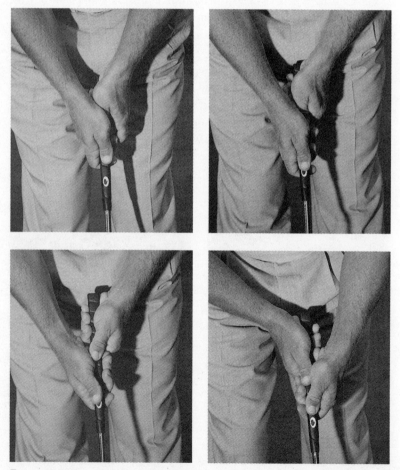

Four common putting grips: conventional, reverse-overlap, split-hand, and left-hand low.

tional grip ruled, but with the success many Tour pros have enjoyed using reverse-overlap (with the left index finger resting in the crevice between the last two fingers of the right hand) and left-hand-low (cross-handed) holds, players now have more options than ever when it comes to gripping their putters. The great German professional Bernhard Langer battled the yips twice in his career. His cure: a switch to a left-hand-low grip in 1985 and an even more unconventional grip in 1993. His reward: two Green Jackets from Augusta National.

Langer's story says a lot about what type of grip a player should use. You have to find the one that feels the best and produces the most desirable results. Below, I've outlined the major grip types and their inherent benefits and restrictions. It's not a bad idea to spend some time experimenting with each. Trial and error will eventually lead you to the perfect hold.

PRIMARY PUTTING GRIPS

TYPE	ELEMENTS	BENEFITS	RESTRICTIONS
Conventional	Most feel and comfort for most players	Familiar feeling, good control of the putterhead	Opportunity for active wrists (and mishits)
Reverse-Overlap	Marries the hands on the grip and creates level shoulders	More control for some players	Less feel for some players
Left-Hand Low	Left shoulder sets up lower and stays lower throughout the stroke	Dead hands (easier to keep the putterhead on-line)	Difficult to take putterhead back far enough on longer putts without dipping the shoulders

Eye Position

The benchmark for putting has always been the professional tours. So it's always a good idea to refer to Tour players when working on your game, whether it's your driver swing, bunker technique, or, as it relates to this book, putting. I spend a lot of time at PGA Tour events, and I've discovered that there are several common denominators in the strokes

What About Grip Pressure?

Far too many golfers, especially amateurs, fail to give the pressure of their grip the attention it deserves. If you grip the putter too tightly, you'll create tension in your stroke, which can lead to acceleration inconsistencies and a lack of distance control. The next time you watch a professional tournament on TV, notice how smoothly the players accelerate the putterhead through the contact zone. It's a constant rate. Gripping the putter too tightly will typically result in a jerky motion, which produces a pop motion rather than the desired, fluid stroke.

On the other hand, a grip that's too loose will fail to provide you with the control so crucial to solid putting. Nevertheless, the right amount of grip pressure should tend toward the light side. Now, be careful here. What I find is that in trying to lighten their grip pressure, most of my amateur students get too loose. The reason is that they focus too much of their attention on their hands. The best way to achieve a nice, light grip pressure is to focus on your forearms.

Take your grip on your putter's handle. Now concentrate on your forearms, specifically the amount of tension within them. Grip the club tightly, and feel the muscles in your forearms contract. Now slowly relax them, to the point where they're tension-free yet your hands are still in control of the putter. Adopting the right grip pressure is as easy as that: relaxed forearms for a relaxed grip. You can't have one without the other.

of the world's best putters. The first of these is that the eyes are positioned directly over, or just slightly inside, the golf ball at address.

There are two lines you need to familiarize yourself with when putting: the target line and the optic line. The target line is an imaginary line that runs through the center of the ball to your target, whether it's the hole, a spot six inches above the ball, or a spike mark a foot in front of the ball—whatever line you're trying to get the ball rolling along. The optic line runs from the point where your eyes contact the ground to the same target. When you can position your optic and target lines in the same plane (i.e., optic line directly on the target line),

A common setup trait of great putters is eyes over the ball. When your eyes are positioned directly over the ball, you'll give yourself the best perspective of the line you plan to putt along and guard against taking the putter back too far to the inside or outside.

you'll give yourself the best perception of the target line from the address position.

Incorrectly positioning the eyes is a serious contributor to putting errors. What's ironic is that with the eyes positioned incorrectly, even the purest of strokes can result in a miss. The problem stems from how our bodies are positioned when we address a golf ball. In other sports, such as basketball or bowling, our eyes point directly toward the target, whether it's the hoop or the 1-pin. In golf, our eyes face perpendicularly away from the target. Golfers have to rotate their heads to see their targets from the address position. The end result is that golfers don't have the luxury of a straight-line perspective. The closest thing to it occurs when the eyes are directly over the golf ball.

When a player addresses a putt with his or her eyes outside the target line, either by crowding the ball or hunching too far over, the dynamics of perspective tell the brain that he or she has aligned the putterface to the right of the target. The body responds by either closing the putterface or stroking the ball with an outside-in motion. The

Setting up to the ball with the eyes positioned either too far to the inside or too far to the outside of the ball line can force a series of errors, including misaligning the clubface and taking the putterhead back either outside (if the eyes are positioned inside the ball) or inside (if the eyes are positioned outside the ball) the target line.

opposite holds true when the eyes are positioned too far to the inside of the ball. The eyes tell the brain that the putterhead is aligned left of the target the golfer has chosen. A common response here is to either open the putterface or putt with an inside-out stroke.

Remember, a key to lights-out putting is consistency. It's much more difficult to achieve consistency if you have to make these sorts of compensations, which can yield decent results in the short run but will otherwise make it difficult for you to putt well day in and day out.

An easy way to train your body to position your eyes over the ball is to address a ball with your normal stance. Take a second ball in your hand and bring it up to the spot directly between your two eye sockets. Let the ball drop. If your eyes are positioned correctly, the second ball should land directly on the ball lying on the ground.

Many instructors use this drill for two reasons: It's simple and very effective. If the second ball lands between your feet and the first ball, you know you've addressed the putt with your eyes positioned too far to the inside. Perform this drill until you can drop the second ball on the first one consistently.

To verify that your eyes are positioned over the ball, perform the Ball-Drop Drill. Address a golf ball, then drop a second from between your eye sockets. If your eyes are positioned correctly, the dropped ball should land directly on the ball on the ground.

Perfect Posture

Addressing a putt with your eyes over the ball will not only give you the most accurate view of your chosen line but can help you build a better putting posture. Of course, there are many more elements of standing correctly to the ball, but what you'll find is that properly positioning your legs, hips, torso, shoulders, and arms begins and ends with eyes over the golf ball.

Good posture is just as important in putting as it is in the full swing. When you stand to the ball with the correct posture, your arms will be free to move during your stroke and your chest will be positioned so that your breathing is easy and natural.

The first step in building proper putting posture is to bend from the hips. Many amateurs bend from the waist, or even the neck and shoulders, creating a posture that not only looks bad but blocks a natural arm hang, as well. You want to bend at your hips just enough to position your eyes directly over the ball and create room for your arms to hang freely and move without resistance during the stroke. It's not a bad idea to perform the ball-drop drill as you experiment with different degrees of hip bend until you can dial in the right amount.

As you ingrain the sensation of bending from the hips, become aware of your shoulder position. Fight the urge to roll your shoulders forward as you bend. Focus on keeping your shoulders back, to the point where it feels as if you're sticking out your chest. If you've been putting with poor posture in the past, it's likely that you'll feel some stress on your lower back. If that's the case, take it easy. Slowly practice this new posture, no more than 10 minutes at a time, while you're on the practice green.

The third key to proper posture is head position. You can destroy a proper hip bend and shoulder placement if your head is positioned incorrectly.

If you're like most amateurs, you confuse eyes over the ball with keeping the head down. That's a recipe for disaster. If your head is positioned too low (i.e., with your chin buried in your

LIGHTS-OUT STAT

At the 1959 U.S. Open, Billy Casper, considered one of the greatest putters of all time, one-putted 31 out of 72 greens at the diabolically fast Winged Foot en route to his first Major victory.

Perfect putting posture dictates that you bend from the hips. When you do, you'll easily be able to position your eyes over the ball and give your arms the room they need to move during the stroke.

Many amateurs slump from the shoulders, creating poor putting posture. Poor posture often blocks your arms and shoulders from making a natural, smooth stroke.

chest), you'll actually bring your shoulders forward and limit the freedom your arms need to move the putter correctly during the stroke.

Instead, keep your head up. Let your eyes focus on the ball. A lights-out putter is a proud putter. Let your head tell the story.

In the fall of 1996, I spent some time in Las Vegas working with David Duval on his putting at the conclusion of Robert Gamez's annual charity golf tournament. The first thing I noticed was that David moved his putter to the inside of the target line (to the left) after impact. This produced one of two errors. If his putterface was square to the path, he'd pull the putt. If his putterface was open to the path, he'd cut across it. David Duval is one of the game's best putters, but sidespin will leave even the best confused. The resultant sidespin from the square-to-inside stroke made it difficult for David to predict the break of a given putt. On a right-to-left putt, the ball would seem to break more than his read if he'd square the face angle to the path. If he happened to open the face to the path, the ball would break less than what he'd read. When a player of David's caliber misses putts in this manner, it often leads the golfer to believe he's misreading his putts.

Considering all of the causes and effects, the most important question was why David swung the putter left through impact. The reason? In his setup position, David's eyes (or optic line) were two to three inches outside the golf ball and his posture was crouched. From this position, David thought he was lined up square to his target, but his putter was actually aimed to the right of the hole. As soon as David took the putter back, his instincts told him he had to swing the putter toward the hole (which was left of where he was aimed) if he wanted to make the putt. That compensating movement—caused by the setup—is what led to the sidespin and the inconsistency in his putting.

After David became aware of his setup tendencies, he lifted his head and shoulders into a better posture and stood a little farther from the ball. This adjustment in his posture positioned his optic line directly on top of his target line. His stroke naturally straightened out, because, with his eyes over the ball, he didn't feel the need to compensate by swinging the putter to the left.

The following summer I worked with Robert Gamez during a practice round before the PGA Championship at Winged Foot. Gamez was paired with Duval, John Daly, and Fuzzy Zoeller. By that time, David had hit a lot of putts from a better setup position, and his stroke looked natural and flowing, with no compensating movements.

Arm Hang

With your eyes over the golf ball and your upper body settled into the perfect posture, it's now time to focus on the placement of your arms, or, more accurately, how your arms hang from your shoulders. The manner in which your arms hang from your shoulders will exert the greatest influence on the path your putterhead takes from and to the ball, which shouldn't be too much of a surprise since, with your wrists taken out of play via the palm grip, the arms are what control the putter.

The ideal placement of the hands and arms is directly underneath the shoulder sockets. If a player sets up with his hands outside (away from the body) his shoulder line, the putterhead will naturally want to

The ideal placement of the hands in the putting setup is directly underneath the shoulders.

swing to the inside of the target line on the backstroke and then outward to get back to the golf ball on the forward stroke. Conversely, if you place your hands inside your shoulder line at address, it will be difficult to move the putterhead anywhere but outside the target line on the backstroke and in toward the ball on the forward stroke. Of course, there are compensations you can make with poor arm and hand positioning and still keep the putterface on-line, but as I said earlier, compensation is the root of all putting evils. You want to be able to putt automatically, not by having to consciously think about manipulating the putterhead with the hands, shoulders, or torso during the stroke. The best strokes are those that happen naturally. Manipulated strokes very rarely produce consistent results.

You can alleviate all of these problems by simply positioning your arms and hands directly underneath your shoulders, which is likely the easiest task in putting since that's where they naturally want to hang. If you've ever watched Greg Norman putt, you've seen him hang his left arm and rock it back and forth before he places his left hand on the put-

A common setup error amateurs commit is setting up with their hands outside their shoulders. From this setup, the putterhead will naturally move to the inside of the target line on the backstroke, which can result in pushes and mishits.

ter. What Norman is trying to accomplish is a natural arm position, one in which his left hand hangs directly underneath his shoulder line.

A by-product of Norman's ritual is less tension in the arms. If your arms are positioned anywhere but directly underneath your shoulders, they'll build more tension than what's needed. Remember, a proper setup is designed to put into motion a smooth, tension-free stroke. Anything else will provide adequate results at best, especially when the heat of the match begins to rise.

Take a moment and perform Norman's preputt arm rock. Stand up, assume your stance, and let your arms hang. Now rock them slightly back and forth. See how they naturally want to settle underneath your shoulder line? Experiment with your arms either too far away from or too close to your body. What you'll find is that as you rock your arms back and forth, they'll always find their natural position. Familiarize yourself with this sensation, because this is how I want your hands and arms to be positioned each and every time you putt.

An Even Weight Distribution

Great putters, once they get their eyes over the ball and position their arms underneath their shoulders, set up so that their lower body balances their upper body. The key word here is *balance*. The underlying theme is an equal distribution of weight, one that stabilizes the upper body during the stroke.

We've established the need for eyes over the ball. Great. Now, what would happen if, taking for granted that the eyes are over the ball, a player's feet were too close to the ball or too far away? In the first situation, the majority of the player's weight will redistribute itself over the heels; in the latter, over the toes. Either way, the player is going to be unbalanced.

At address, it's common for players to feel balanced even though their weight distribution is unequal. The reason is that the putter is resting on the ground. In simple terms, when a player is unbalanced as he is at address, the putterhead will actually serve as a crutch. Now, what do you think happens when the putter is put into motion? Well, if your weight is on your toes, and your "crutch" is removed, you'll naturally feel the weight imbalance and move backward to regain your sense of balance. The opposite holds true if you set up with your weight distributed more toward your heels.

If your body moves during the stroke, the chances of your keeping the putterhead on-line are going to drop like a lead balloon. The chances of mishitting a putt on the heel or toe, on the other hand, are going to drastically increase.

Players who putt well agree that the head must stay still during the putting stroke. That's why setting up with the proper weight distribution is so important. As you stand to the ball, concentrate on the distribution of weight over your feet. You should feel as if the entire soles of both feet support the weight of your upper body equally. If you have difficulty feeling the distribution of weight, practice by gripping down an extra inch on the putter grip and hover the putterhead above the ground so it can't act like a crutch. Set your posture as you've learned so that your eyes are over the ball and your hands are underneath your shoulders. Once in that position, inch your feet closer to the ball until you notice that your weight is firmly over your heels. Now inch your feet away from the ball until you feel the majority of your weight settle over your toes. After you become aware of both extremes, adjust your feet until you sense an even weight distribution, with neither too little nor too much weight distrib-

The final element of setting up to the ball correctly is establishing an even weight distribution. You'll discover this balanced state when your hips are positioned over the soles of your feet. If you stand too close or too far away you'll create an uneven weight distribution, leading to instability, and risk the chance of moving the putterhead off-line during the stroke.

uted over your toes or heels. Only by becoming aware of the two weight distribution extremes will you be able to find your true, balanced center.

POOR SETUP CONSEQUENCES

EYES	WEIGHT DISTRIBUTION	ARMS	RESULT (IN RELATION TO TARGET)
Inside golf ball	Over heels	Outside shoulders	Push right (or compensate to left)
Outside golf ball	Over toes	Inside shoulders	Pull left (or compensate to right)
Over golf ball	Even	Under shoulders	On-target

Fringe Setup Elements

To make the five main elements of the proper putting setup come together—proper grip, eyes over the ball, correct posture, arms underneath the shoulders, balanced weight distribution—you're going to need the right putter. Specifically, you need to find the right length for your putter. As we'll see in Chapter 4, improper putter length can make setting up properly nearly impossible. Imagine putting with a 10-inch putter. You can picture yourself hunched over, eyes outside the ball and your weight over your toes. That's a dramatic example, but even an inch in the wrong direction can inflict serious damage to your setup.

Ball Position

A frequently asked question I hear from my students is "Where should I play the ball in my stance?" As you can guess, there's not one correct answer here. Ball position is dictated by personal preference. As a general rule, however, I advocate playing the ball slightly forward of the putterhead when the puttershaft is in-line with the center of the sternum. The reason I favor setting up with the puttershaft in the middle of the sternum is that it's here where the putter will bottom out during the stroke and where impact should occur. Playing the ball slightly forward of this position will increase the chances of hitting the ball on the upstroke. Playing the ball behind this position will increase the chances of hitting the ball on the downstroke.

Shoulder Alignment

As far as your shoulders are concerned, we know that they must serve
as the reference point for your arms to hang under. But in order to
make the whole system work, you need to make sure that your shoulder line runs parallel to your target line. Amateurs, the majority of
whom can't resist the temptation to watch the ball to see where it's
headed as soon as contact is made, tend to set up with their shoulder
lines open to the target (pointing left for a right-handed golfer). If
you're guilty of this, you've probably noticed that the majority of your
putts roll left of your targets or that you cut a fair share of your putts.
Putting with open shoulders produces the same results as it does in the
full swing: a pull (if the face is square) or a slice (if the face is left open).

The best way to see if your shoulders are positioned properly is to
work in front of a mirror. Only a side view will show any errors, if they
exist. Check to see that your hip and shoulder lines run parallel to the
target line.

*Where should you play the ball in
your stance? Just ahead of the putterhead when the shaft is aligned with
the middle of your sternum.*

*Be careful not to set up with your
shoulders open to the target line.
Open shoulders can force you to pull
your putts or, if the face is left open,
send them spinning off to the right.*

As part of your putting practice, check your body lines in front of a mirror. Verify that your shoulder line, putterface, hips, and toe line (if you putt with a square stance) point along lines that run parallel to your target line.

Square, Open, or Closed?

In the spirit of comfort, I give my students freedom to position their feet to suit their preferences. What I've discovered over the years is that many players feel more comfortable putting from a slightly open stance. Some prefer a closed stance, but on the whole, most prefer to putt with their left, or lead, foot turned toward the target. Tom Watson advocated an open stance, with his front foot flared 10 degrees from the target line. If you like to putt with an open stance, go for it. But remember, don't allow your shoulders to open along with your stance. More important, remember to move the putter along your target line, not your toe line. Many of my students who putt with an open stance fall into the habit of stroking the ball along a line that runs parallel to their toe line, which, in the case of an open stance, is wide left of the target.

I know I've given you a lot of material to digest, but it's not complicated if you take it in steps: grip, eyes, arms, and weight. If you practice these fundamentals, you'll lay the foundation for a mechanically correct putting stroke.

Nevertheless, you can't afford to take the requirements of the putting setup for granted. After all, the setup dictates the success or failure of every putt. In fact, its importance is so great that I often ask my more ambitious students to practice their setup not once or twice a week, but every day.

3

The Lights-Out Stroke

You can tell a good putt by the noise it makes.
—Bobby Locke

Green reading is a science. So, too, is setting up to the ball properly. Likewise for finding the right putter. The stroke? Well, that's an entirely different science altogether. It's a sweet science, one that combines physical facts and—to use the term loosely—"physical fiction."

I use the word "fiction" because many golfers, in executing their putting strokes, leave everything to the imagination. You've seen these players. They're the ones with the flying elbows (à la Leo Diegel, the back-to-back PGA champ) and the bowed knees (à la George Archer). I love the fact that players adopt personal putting styles. All the great players do. During the 1960s, three of the top putters on tour were known for three unique putting strokes. Billy Casper, considered one of the greatest putters of all time, was all wrists. Arnold Palmer, who never let a putt die before it got to the hole, was all hands. And Jack Nicklaus, noted for his familiar crouch, was predominately a shoulder-oriented putter. Three champions, three different strokes. Obviously, where putting is concerned, there's a lot of room for personal expression.

This should be good news for the recreational golfer. In fact, it's great news. The putting stroke provides you with the opportunity to do whatever feels good and makes you comfortable. Most important, it will allow you to putt instinctively, leaving your mind clear and free to focus on the target.

Now, I'm not giving you the green light to move your putter in any manner and in any direction. There are certain things you must do when putting that are absolute necessities. However, these "musts" lack the stringency of the "musts" of the full swing. I've always found this to be quite ironic, for it's on the putting green where there's the least room for error. Nevertheless, it's true.

Putting is delicate. Putting is exact. Furthermore, putting involves not only distance and direction, but speed, as well. Do you ever think about how hard to hit your driver? Probably not. You just swing away and "let 'er rip." But you do concern yourself with how hard you hit your putts—all your putts. This is where your sense of feel takes over. Feel is an intangible asset that enables a player to gauge just how hard or soft to hit a given putt, taking into consideration all of the varying external factors, such as the speed of the greens, the slope, and whether or not the putting surface has been watered.

In our discussion of the putting stroke in this chapter, I'll continually bring up the feel element of putting. Although guidelines will be presented, I want you to develop your own personal stroke. A lights-out putter shouldn't hone a stroke based solely on rules. A lights-out putter uses a stroke that provides confidence, is reliable, and generates the best results.

Before the Stroke: The Lights-Out Preputt Routine

The act of putting is a play with two acts: The Setup and The Stroke. Here is where the action lies. But just like a good play, the acts need to relate. This is what makes the preputt routine—the link between the setup and stroke—so important. It blends the physical and mental preparations that allow you to make a smooth, comfortable stroke.

Time and again I hear Tour professionals comment that, when the going gets tough, it's their preputt routines that pull them through. In professional golf, there are many things that are out of a player's control. The preputt routine shouldn't be one of them. In that respect alone, a finely tuned, familiar preputt routine can be a golfer's best friend.

Below you'll find an example of a complete preputt routine. It's the one I offer my students, and it's what I use when I'm playing, as well. In my opinion, your preputt should include all of these steps. Yet the need to make your preputt routine yours and yours only remains. For ideas, watch the professionals on TV and see if you can pick up additional steps that may work in your favor. Then design a routine that can

Read the putt.   *Take your stance.*   *Take dead aim.*

Take a final look.   *Trust and let it go.*

easily be remembered. A characteristic of a good preputt routine is that it can be easily repeated from memory.

- **Read the putt.** First from behind the ball and then from the low side of hole; if you can't get a good read, then take a third look from behind the hole.

- **Find the breaking point.** From behind the ball, the point where the putt will reach its apex before turning toward the cup
- **Choose an intermediate target.** Along the target line, roughly 12 inches in front of the ball
- **Move to the side of the ball.**
- **Take practice strokes (if you prefer).** With an eye toward matching the length of the backstroke to the length of the putt
- **Align the putterhead to the target.** Only the putterhead at this point
- **Set body lines, posture, arm hang, and stance.** Hips and shoulders parallel to target line, eyes over ball, arms under shoulders
- **Relaxed breathing.** Calming inhales and exhales before your stroke
- **Final look, target visualization.** Your last look—burn the target into your mind's eye
- **Eyes back to the ball, trust, and let go.**

Remember, in designing your preputt routine, it's important to do so with an eye toward repeatability. You should be able to perform your preputt routine during a match as easily as you can when you practice. The key is consistency, developed through practice.

Different Strokes

The game of golf is in a constant state of change. All you have to do is look at today's equipment and compare it to the clubs you played with five years ago and you'll realize that, in this game, things rarely stay the same. The same is true with the golf swing, especially where putting is concerned.

In the '40s, '50s, and even the '60s, the wristy putting stroke was the dominant putting motion. Players like Snead, Locke, De Vicenzo and others made Hall of Fame careers out of such a stroke. If you catch any of the old reruns on TV or were lucky enough to watch these players in their prime, you understand how the wrist, or "pop," stroke works. Basically, to start the motion, the player cocks the putterhead back by hinging the right wrist (for a right-handed golfer). The exact amount of wrist cock varies—it all depends on the length of the putt. On the forward stroke, the putterhead is brought back to the hitting zone by hinging the wrists in the opposite direction so that, at the finish, the left wrist

The wristy putting stroke dominated the game through the 1960s. In the wristy stroke, also known as the pop stroke, the putter is set into motion by the hinging and unhinging of the wrists, the dynamics of which help the ball rise before rolling end over end. The wristy stroke can work well on slow or bumpy greens, but is inherently difficult to control for most amateurs.

is cupped and the right wrist is flat or slightly bowed. To facilitate this type of motion, players typically grip the putter in their fingers. A finger grip gives the wrists freedom to hinge and unhinge.

The wristy putting stroke is hardly a fluid motion. It's not necessarily a jab motion, either. But it does put an interesting hit on the ball. The uncocking of the wrists at impact produces a little "pop"—hence the term "pop stroke." The ball literally jumps off the putterface before it begins rolling end over end toward the target. Sounds inconsistent, doesn't it? Well, it is, but so were the greens on the majority of the courses players competed on during the early years of professional golf. The pop was needed to overcome bumps, rises, and severe grain inherent with the greens of old. The great Sam Snead has quipped that today's fairways are better conditioned than yesteryear's greens, which were also much slower. The pop stroke worked best on these types of greens.

A problem arose as soon as conditions improved. The major limitation of a wristy putting stroke is that it's hard to control. In the pop stroke, it's the little muscles that do the majority of the work, and it's inherently more difficult for a player to control the smaller muscles than the big ones. As greens became faster, it was obvious that the pop stroke had seen its day. But its legacy still lives. In fact, if you frequently play on municipal greens, or if the greens at your home course are particularly slow, then you might want to give the wristy putting stroke a try. I'm not a big fan of the wristy putting stroke, but I do understand that it's a legitimate way to putt successfully in certain situations. Yet, with the goal of lights-out putting in mind, the pop stroke isn't your best bet, especially on the well-manicured greens of today.

The initial reaction to the demise of the wristy putting stroke was the development of the shoulder stroke. The term "shoulder stroke" shouldn't be confused with the phrase "pendulum putting stroke." The shoulder stroke is simply that: a stroke that responds solely to the movement of the shoulders. Although a pendulum stroke involves the shoulders, it's not a shoulder stroke in the exact sense of the word (as you'll soon discover).

The problem I see in a pure shoulder stroke is that it allows the putterhead to rise on the backstroke. This may be hard to visualize, so think of it this way: at address, the putter lies in a unique position in relation to the shoulders, somewhere close to exactly in between them, and retains this position throughout the stroke. To keep the putterhead in between the shoulders, a player must dip the left shoulder (for a right-handed golfer) on the backstroke. The same occurs in the forward

Spike Impact

Better chemicals, better mowers, and better drainage systems have enabled modern greenskeepers to groom putting surfaces as smooth as glass. But recently, the number-one contributor to green health has been the spikeless—or plastic-spiked—golf shoe.

No less than 10 years ago, shoes equipped with 7mm metal spikes were the norm. While the soles of these shoes provided ample support for the full swing, they weren't friendly to the greens. Amateurs and professionals alike had to deal with spike marks on the putting surface, the smallest of which could send even the most perfectly struck putt off-line.

Beginning in 1995, a revolution started, spearheaded by Softspikes, the Maryland-based cleat company. Their plastic spike, which provided decent traction but damaged greens far less than their metal counterparts, ushered in the "no-spike" policy, whereby courses outlawed any shoe with metal spikes. Since then, more than 20,000 courses have instituted a "no metal spike" policy.

This has affected golfers in two ways. One, it has forced them to outfit their shoes with plastic spikes or purchase one of the ever-growing number of spikeless shoe models. Two, it has all but removed spike marks from the greens. So, not only are today's greens faster than ever, they're devoid of bruises and scars from metal spikes, as well. To most experts, this is a benefit to all parties. The lone negative: no longer can golfers blame a spike mark for a missed two-footer.

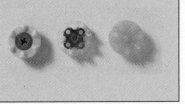

stroke, where the right shoulder must dip in order to accelerate the putterhead through the hitting zone and into the finish.

The shoulder stroke became popular for one main reason: it affords players the ability to better control the direction of their putts. Remember what I said about larger muscles being easier to control than smaller ones? But because the putterhead has to rise on the backstroke, bottom out, and rise on the forward stroke, executing the shoulder

As its name suggests, the shoulder stroke is powered by the movement of the shoulders. Although the shoulder stroke can make it easier to keep the ball on line, the rising and dropping of the putterhead makes perfect contact with the ball difficult, resulting in poor control of speed.

stroke requires expert skill to contact the ball on its equator with the exact center of the putterface. Catch the ball on the upswing and it will bounce upward. Catch it with a descending arc and it will drive into the turf. Both types of contact will make it difficult to put a consistent roll on the ball, resulting in a loss of distance and speed control.

Finding Your Putter's Center

In the perfectly executed putting stroke, the ball is struck on its equator with the center of the putterface. This center, or sweet spot, varies from putter to putter, and is not often located in the exact center of the putterface.

To find your putter's sweet spot, simply dangle the putter between your thumb and forefinger, letting it hang freely. With your free forefinger, begin tapping the putter at various spots along the face until the putter rebounds straight back without twisting or turning. The point at which you applied the tap is your putter's center. It's a good idea to mark where this sweet spot lies either with a pen or by etching a notch on the top edge of your putter.

Which brings us to the main requirement of the stroke: you need to hit the ball in its center with the center of your putterface while it remains square to the target line through the hitting zone. Anything else is a mishit, a malady as ruinous to your game as a poor read, a faulty setup, or a lack of confidence. Your putting stroke should result in perfect contact every time. That's the true goal of putting. If you can develop a putting motion that allows you to make perfect contact with the ball consistently, then you're well on your way to becoming a lights-out putter.

The great putters of the past weren't great putters because they knew certain stroke secrets or had developed radical new techniques that left the rest of the field scratching their heads. Every player was subject to the shortcomings of the wristy and shoulder strokes. What made some players better than others was, sure, their athletic skill, but also their dedication to practice and to perfecting their strokes. They learned to make perfect contact every time: center of the putter on the center of the ball without fail.

As a recreational golfer, it may not be feasible for you to put in the long practice hours needed to achieve this sort of mastery, especially with the types of strokes discussed thus far. For the weekend golfer, there are too many things that can go wrong with the wristy putting stroke or

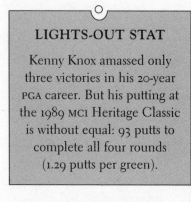

the shoulder stroke, despite their inherent assets. The same holds true for the majority of players on tour today, who, like the amateur, want nothing more than consistent, solid contact from their putter every time they stand over the ball. That's why you see so many professionals using an arm stroke. Brad Faxon, Jim Furyk, and other modern-day greats employ such a stroke. And it's the one I'd like you to give a committed try, as well.

The Arm Stroke

The primary key to a really good arm stroke is understanding that the stroke is controlled by the arms. The shoulders will move, but only as a result of the movement of the arms. Everything else needs to remain completely still, from your feet on up. So it's important that you develop a stroke center—a stable point from which your arms can swing. You'll notice that as you putt with the arm stroke, your arms will actually separate from the body. In the shoulder stroke or wrist stroke, the arms stay on your sides. In the arm stroke, your right arm will separate from your right hip on the backstroke, and as you move through to the finish, your left arm will move away from your left hip. This needed separation can occur only if you build a solid platform to swing from, which is why you need to focus on your head—and especially your sternum—and keep them as centered as possible.

A good drill to instill the feeling of arm separation in the arm stroke is to putt with only one hand, either the right or the left. Simply move the putterhead back and through, focusing on the feeling of the arm you're using separating from your body's center (on the backstroke with the right arm and on the forward stroke with the left arm). Practice this feeling and make it your own—it will pay dividends when you put the complete stroke to use. At the 1999 Canadian Open, I witnessed six professionals over a two-hour period practice this drill, including Nick Faldo.

A second key to a really good arm stroke, and to developing the feel of using your arms to propel the putterhead, is first to get rid of all the

For most amateurs, the arm stroke will provide the most consistent results. The primary key to a good arm stroke is allowing the arms to separate from the hips. For this to occur, your head and sternum must be centered and stable.

tension in your upper body. The best way to do this is to go through a series of relaxed inhales and exhales. There's no need to exaggerate your breathing. Just take a nice, slow inhale deep into your lungs and a nice, slow exhale. As you exhale, feel the tension in your upper body and arms relax and let go.

A third key to the arm stroke is dictated by your setup. Recall the emphasis I placed on adopting a setup in which the hands hang directly underneath the shoulder line and the shoulders are aligned parallel to the target line. Setting up with the hands under the shoulders and the shoulders pointed in the same direction you want to putt tells your mind and body to give your arms the "go" signal and begin the putting motion. When one of the Tour players I work with begins to falter on the greens, I always look at his setup. Often, he has his shoulders pointed open or closed, or has moved his hands inside or outside his shoulder line. This sends subtle signals to the mind that something's not right. Tension builds, and confidence and trust in the arms to control the stroke rightfully drops. When the setup is wrong, the need to compensate increases while the consistency of impact decreases.

Putt with only one hand to instill the feeling of proper arm movement in a fundamentally correct arm stroke.

Inside, Outside, On-Line?

When talking about the stroke, instructors harp on the fact that the putterhead must move along the target line throughout the impact area in order for a golfer to realize consistent results. And they're exactly right. What they don't often talk about is that if you set up with your arms underneath your shoulders, and position your shoulders correctly, all you have to do is move your arms. A golfer shouldn't worry about the putterhead during the stroke, or how it should be manipulated to make square contact with the ball at impact. When your setup is correct, all you have to do is move your arms.

Over the years, much has been made of certain stroke paths. I'm sure you've read somewhere that this or that pro uses an "inside-square-inside" putting stroke, as if it's something radical and different from the arm stroke we're discussing here. It's not. It's simply that some golfers, mainly those with the luxury of abundant practice time and above-average skill, allow the putterhead to drift to the inside of the target line on the takeaway. That's certainly okay. The most important thing to remember about stroke path is that the putterhead must move along the target line as it travels through the impact area. That's why I advo-

Some golfers advocate taking the putterhead straight back. Others support a path that's slightly inside the target line on the takeaway. The most important thing to remember about path is that the putterhead must travel along the target line as it moves through the impact area.

cate taking the putterhead back and through along as straight a line as possible, especially on short putts.

However, on longer putts, where you need to increase the length of your backstroke to roll the ball the appropriate distance, you'll find the putterhead will want to travel slightly inside on the backstroke. (In my opinion, this isn't an inside-square-inside stroke. You're simply allowing the putterhead to move naturally.) Don't fight the putter's inherent tendencies. If, on a longer stroke, you try to keep the putterhead on-line, you'll manipulate your hand or shoulder position. And that's just another error you'll need to correct in order to make the type of contact that produces the best roll.

Acceleration, Rhythm, and Tempo

One thing that's often misunderstood and/or miscommunicated is the element of acceleration, or, to be more specific, overacceleration. When one of your putts comes up short, more often than not you or one of your partners will diagnose the error as a failure to accelerate through the ball. In reality, a putt that comes up short is a result of a mishit. What I've learned over the years is that most players, regardless of experience, understand that they must accelerate through the putt. And the majority of golfers putt with needed acceleration, but they mis-strike the ball, hitting up into it, down into it, hitting it off the toe, etc.

Diagnosing mishits as acceleration failure will eventually force a player to overaccelerate, especially on short putts, resulting in mishit putts that are hit too hard. In the short run, this type of overcompensation can work with some success. I'll bet you can recall at least a dozen putts you stroked that felt "bad" but still managed to find the bottom of the cup. That's the feeling of overhitting a mishit.

If the process continues, a player will develop a stroke characterized by a short backstroke and jerky forward stroke, a type of arm-pop stroke. Compare this type of stroke to the ones you see players such as Ernie Els and Mark O'Meara use. These are fluid, rhythmic motions. They have proper tempo. They have constant acceleration. If you've fallen into the habits described above, it's safe to say that on some putts, especially those that mean something, you may fall prey to the yips. The yips—yes, they are for real—are nothing more than a lack of rhythm and tempo, which is exactly what you'll develop if you compensate for mishits by overaccelerating.

Stroke Length

Over time, the players with the smoothest strokes and with the most constant tempo will reap the rewards a made putt can provide. The same goes for those who use a short backstroke only for short putts and a longer stroke only for lengthy putts, and who match the lengths of their backstrokes with the lengths of their forward strokes. Amateurs are often guilty of using the same length stroke for each and every putt, whether it's a two-footer or 40-footer. They adjust for the length by changing the force of their stroke. That's another tempo-breaker. You need to adjust for the length of the putt by altering the length of your stroke, and maintain the same tempo. That builds rhythm, which you'll need if you want consistent results like the pros.

The key to all of this is to keep it simple. The more you get caught up in mechanics, the more pressure you'll put on your body and mind. You'll invite tension into your stroke and you'll lose your target aware-ness. By the time you finish this book, and practice the instruction I've

A key to a sound putting stroke is matching the length of your backstroke with the length of your forward stroke.

provided, I want you to be able to perform your preputt routine, settle into your stance, and execute your stroke without having to think about any of the physical requirements of each. Once you can do this, you can shift your focus to your target. Your target is all that truly matters. Hitting to it is the only way you'll consistently make putts. The last thought I want in your head is not how far back to take the putterhead, but where your target is, what it looks like, and how the ball is going to find it and drop into the cup. That type of focus means you need to clear your head of any stroke-related thoughts.

A Few Keys

In regard to the stroke itself, the arm stroke in particular, there are only a few keys. So it shouldn't take too much to master them and free up your mind to perform the task at hand. If you can accomplish the following, you'll be just fine:

- Rid your upper body of tension.
- Secure your head and chest.
- Move the putter with your arms.
- Ingrain the feeling of arm separation.

- Stroke along the target line.
- Match stroke length with the length of the putt.
- Match backstroke length with forward stroke length.
- Think rhythm and tempo.
- Think rhythm and tempo.
- Think rhythm and tempo.

The last three requirements, as you no doubt noticed, are repeated. That's because they're the most crucial elements of the stroke. Remember the feel element of putting discussed earlier in this chapter? Well, to develop a feel for putting, you need to have the right tempo in your stroke. Many players on the Tour are now using metronomes or similar timing devices (available at most music stores) when they practice their putting. You might consider this strange behavior, but it shows the importance of tempo in the putting stroke. The great Tom Watson often practiced his stroke by counting, out loud even: "One" on the backstroke, "two" on the forward stroke. Watson always said that anyone who could count to two could make a smooth putting stroke.

A lights-out putter doesn't hit putts. He strokes them—with the same force and speed every time. Again, adjusting for speed and break should begin and end with adjusting the length of the backstroke. It's that easy folks, a task that can become second nature with practice, patience, and perseverance.

Flaws and Fixes

The act of putting is so precise that it's easy to fall into bad habits. Even the greatest putters with the smoothest strokes will allow faults to creep into their setup and stroke that go undiagnosed for a period of time until their scores start to rise. Amateurs are prey to the same scenario, which is why you need to practice a lot of putts to see what your tendencies are. Do most of your putts miss to the left? Do most of your putts come up short? Answering these questions may provide a quick route to improvement, especially if your stroke is otherwise fundamentally sound.

The Yips

As we saw earlier, the most common error players commit when putting is combining mishitting with an overaccelerating stroke, and

BRAD FAXON—A LIGHTS-OUT PUTTER

From 1991 to 1998, Brad Faxon ranked in the Top 10 in putting on the PGA Tour four times. He's been able to put up great putting numbers throughout his career, including an average of 1.73 putts per green in regulation, largely because of a positive mental attitude. He believes he can make every putt he looks at, but accepts that not every good stroke will yield the desired results.

In addition to his mental toughness, Faxon also utilizes an outstanding ability to read greens as well as a near-perfect address position to make sure he rolls the ball on the proper line. With his eyes directly over the ball, Faxon keeps his head perfectly still throughout the stroke, never looking up prematurely, and always striking the ball on its equator. Like many great putters, Faxon keeps his shoulders square and lets his forearms control the stroke. This facilitates a one-piece motion in which the triangle formed by his shoulders, arms, and hands is maintained throughout the stroke.

Fax, as he's known on the Tour, hasn't bagged many victories (only five in more than 400 events through 1999), but his lights-out stroke consistently keeps him in the hunt. In fact, he's finished in the Top 25 in almost half of the tournaments in which he makes the cut, a consistency that's paid him nearly $7 million dollars in earnings since he turned pro in 1983.

developing a short backstroke with a hard, rocky forward stroke. In my opinion, these faults invariably lead to the yips. Anyone who has experienced the yips knows just how frustrating the game of golf can become. But there's hope. Many of the world's best players have overcome the yips to win Major championships later in their careers.

The key to practicing out of the yips is a very smooth acceleration and removing all tension from the arms, given that the fundamentals of the setup are correct. If everything is lined up correctly and the putter fits the player, then the yips come down to an issue of tempo and acceleration.

A good drill to improve the acceleration aspect of your putting, and to beat the yips, is to drop a couple of quarters on the green, one six inches behind the ball and one six inches in front of the ball. Practice your stroke, making sure to move the putterhead to the back quarter and stopping it at the forward quarter, or slightly past it. This will teach you to match the length of your backstroke to the length of your forward stroke. Matching stroke lengths is key if you want to develop proper tempo. You won't ever build the fluidity necessary for successful putting if your backstroke doesn't match your forward stroke. Vary the distance of the quarters, moving them as far back and as far in front of the ball as 18 inches.

Another yip-causing flaw for many players is a right-hand grip pressure that's too tight. As outlined in Chapter 2, grip pressure should be the same in both hands, and the palms, not the fingers, should control the club. If your right-hand grip pressure is too strong, or if you grip the club with your fingers, the right wrist can get too active, making it difficult to control the putterface—specifically, how far back and through you take it. The only way you'll ever be able to consistently control your stroke length is by letting the big muscles in your arms and shoulders take over. Otherwise, you're likely to develop a back/forward stroke mismatch and inconsistent acceleration.

Pushes

If your putts typically miss to the right, perform this test to discover the root of the problem. Place two tees about six inches behind the ball and far enough apart so that your putter can just squeeze between them—a type of gate. Now make your back stroke. If the heel of your putter catches the inside tee, it's likely that you're coming into the ball with an inside-out stroke. This will force the putt to the right. The fix: work on your setup and make sure that your hands are positioned directly underneath your shoulders. If the putterhead passes through the gate cleanly, and you still manage to push the ball, it's possible that you're dipping the right shoulder on the forward stroke, swinging into the ball on an upward arc, which opens the face and sends the ball in

If the heel of your putter catches the inside tee in the Gate Drill, then your stroke is prone to produce pushes (if the face remains square to the path) and pulls (if the face closes in relation to the path).

the wrong direction. This is called "coming out" of the putt. If this is the case, then you've got to work on letting your arms finish the putt—specifically, allowing your lead arm to separate from the body on the forward stroke. I don't care how short a putt is—if you come out of it, you'll risk the chance of sliding by the hole.

Pulls

Pulls are discouraging because, at impact, they often feel really good. Most pulled putts are hit in the center of the putterface. The problem stems mostly from the setup and not the stroke. If you set up with your hands below your shoulder line, you'll bring the putter to the outside as it swings back. On the forward stroke, the putter has nowhere to go but back to the inside. This outside-in stroke, much like an outside-in swing, will result in a pull if the face is square to the path.

A more common mistake, and probably the one that afflicts 90 percent of golfers who pull their putts, is setting up to the ball with the shoulders pointed left of the target. This flaw is easy to commit, because golfers like to look to the area where all the action is—the hole—and they set up with their shoulders and upper body open to the target. If a player makes a natural stroke from this position, the putt will drift left of the hole.

There's a famous story about Jack Nicklaus at the 1966 Masters. On the 71st hole, he pulled a straight three-footer left of the hole. It didn't even catch an edge. The miss pulled him into a tie with Tommy Jacobs and Gay Brewer. Luckily, Nicklaus was able to overcome his mistake and win the tournament in a playoff. A befuddled Nicklaus later caught his disastrous putt on TV tape and gasped as the bird's-eye view showed him setting up several inches left of the hole.

Nicklaus's example illustrates the importance of the setup fundamentals. You can never take them for granted. If you feel you pull a fair share of your putts, go directly to your setup. I'm sure you'll find the cure there.

Distance Control

Distance control is what typically limits the mid- to high-handicap golfer from performing his or her best. It takes time to develop the feel necessary to match stroke length with putt distance. If you experience distance-control problems because, let's face it, you haven't learned how big a stroke to make to roll the ball 20 feet versus what it takes to

Charge or Die?

While there are many putting stances, grips, and strokes to choose from, there are basically only two putting styles: "charge" or "die." The method you choose has a lot to do with your natural tempo and instinct. In his prime, Arnold Palmer was considered the greatest charge putter of all time. He aggressively attacked every putt, trying to hit the back of the hole hard enough to ensure that the ball would rebound into the bottom of the cup. At his best, Tom Watson was also an excellent charge putter who made bold runs at the hole without the fear of missing or facing a tough comebacker.

Jack Nicklaus and Ben Crenshaw are two great putters who preferred the die method—trying to drop the ball just over the front or side of the cup with perfect speed. Although this style demands greater touch and green-reading ability, it tends to produce shorter comebackers and less three-putts. The die method also helps develop a better sense of distance control, which can be helpful on all short-game shots.

In my opinion, you should adapt your stroke to the type of putt you're faced with. If you have a slick, breaking downhill putt, then die the ball into the hole. If you have an uphill putt, or are playing on slow greens, then charge the hole.

roll the ball seven feet, don't be disappointed when I say that you won't find an answer to your problems here. Unfortunately, there isn't a magic formula in putting that says for an 18-foot putt, take the putterhead back 10 inches. Such a thing just doesn't exist. All I can recommend is that you build a repertoire of stroke lengths by practicing putts of various distances from various lies.

If you can never seem to dial in the correct distance, your control problems represent a new set of errors altogether. The same goes if on one day you can never get to the cup and the next you're blowing it three and four feet by the hole. If this sounds like you, then it's likely that you're adding or subtracting loft from what's built into your putterface (four degrees has proven optimal at impact). Every putter is built with a certain degree of loft. If you come into the ball on an ascending arc, you'll add loft to the putter, causing the ball to rise more than usual and reduce the distance that it would travel had you hit it squarely. If you come into the ball with a descending arc, you'll subtract loft from the putterface. The typical result of this scenario is that the ball travels farther than normal.

A compound problem arises if you add loft to the club, realize all of your putts are coming up short, and then add some force to your stroke. Here's where distance control can really turn your hair gray. You'll never know how far your putts travel unless you can learn to consistently strike the ball squarely with the amount of loft that's built into your putterface. That's why I don't advocate the shoulder stroke. The putterhead, with its rise in the backstroke and fall in the forward stroke, makes it too easy to change the loft of the face as contact with the ball is made. The arm stroke, performed correctly, ensures that you strike the ball with the right amount of loft. The key is to keep the putterhead low to the ground throughout the entire stroke. If the height of your putter varies throughout your putting motion, you're only asking for trouble. Unless you have robotlike reflexes, you'll hit most of your putts with different degrees of putterface loft, making the task of controlling the distance of your putts nearly impossible.

4

Choosing the Right Putter

Golf is a game whose aim is to hit a very small ball into a very small hole, with weapons singularly ill-designed for that purpose.
—Winston Churchill

Except for auto racing, golf may be the most equipment-driven sport ever devised. For years, centuries even, manufacturers have searched for the right materials, head shapes, and shaft geometries to help you and the other members of your foursome better enjoy the game. And to a certain degree, they've done a pretty fair job. All you have to do is watch a mid-handicapper blast a 275-yard drive (which would have led the Tour driving-distance category as recently as 1985) to realize that today's equipment provides little room for improved performance.

That said, it should come as no surprise that most of the drivers and iron sets in your local pro shop are similar in appearance. This homogeneity exists because manufacturers have pretty much dialed in the head shapes and sizes that work best when subjected to the forces of a fundamentally sound golf swing. Any experienced club designer will tell you that the next step in driver and iron construction will take the form of weight distribution, new materials, and advanced custom fitting, not so much a redesign of how today's clubs look.

It's a different story altogether with putters, where you'll be hard-pressed to find two that look exactly alike (although there are certain "proven" putter designs that are widely copied). The reason why putters have so many different forms is that, as we learned in Chapter 3, there's ample room for personal expression when putting. Remember, putting is personal, and dependent as much on how you're built as it is on how you move the putterhead from address through the impact zone. The challenge to manufacturers is to develop new designs, new materials, and new optics to fit what's basically a never-ending pool of putting styles.

Obviously, the goal of this book is to help you improve your putting skills. While learning and practicing the appropriate techniques will go a long way toward helping you sink more putts, you'll never reach your true potential unless you find the putter that maximizes your stroke and, more important, matches your physical characteristics. The only way to effectively do this is to become familiar with the key elements of putter design. By doing a little homework, you'll better your chances of finding the putter perfect for you. Otherwise, you're bound to end up with a closetful of putters that simply don't work.

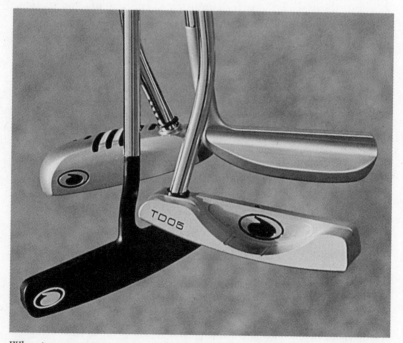

When it comes to putters, manufacturers must constantly look toward new designs and materials to complement the wide variety of stroke and feel preferences of today's players.

Fit Your Setup

How did you select the putter that's currently in your bag? If you're like most golfers, you probably walked into a golf shop and pulled a few putters off the rack that "looked good" to you, or that you heard were "great" or were used by your favorite Tour players. You likely putted a few trial putts and, if a few dropped, slapped down the credit card and walked away with a new putter. All I can say about this purchasing method is that it's one way to purchase a putter. But it's not the right way.

The putter that's going to work best for you won't always come off the rack. Just like a nice suit, you must make sure that a putter fits you and your putting posture, not vice versa. If a putter doesn't fit your posture, it will force you to make compensations in your stroke. And the last thing you want to worry about when standing over a must-make five-footer are undue compensations.

If you're serious about finding a new putter, you must first get in touch with your setup fundamentals. How you position your body when you address a putt lays the blueprints for deciding which types of putters will perform best for you. The absolute most important aspect of choosing a putter is finding one that helps you set up to the ball correctly. The design and balance of a putter should complement your stroke preferences, but such customization is secondary to the importance of finding a putter that features the right specs for your physique when you stand over a putt using the three basic rules of putting posture: eyes over the ball, hands underneath shoulders, even weight distribution.

When it comes to putters, one size—or one style—doesn't fit all. Therefore, it's imperative that you discover what length and lie values are right for you. Once you do, you can apply these values to any style of putter that looks good to you and fits your stroke and feel preferences.

Lies and Lengths

The lie of a putter is indicated by the angle formed by the shaft line and the ground. Find two similar putters with different lie angles and take your address position with each. As you do, you'll notice that each positions your hands differently in your setup if you keep the putterhead flat on the ground. The more upright putter will move your hands higher than normal, while the flatter putter will position your hands lower than normal.

The lie of a putter is the angle formed between the puttershaft and the ground. In relation to your physique, different lie angles can produce putters that are too flat or too upright.

Never allow the lie of a putter to dictate where you place your hands, which, as indicated by the second rule of putting posture, should be directly below your shoulders.

When you grip a putter in your hands, make sure that the sole of the putter rests perfectly flat on the putting surface. If, after taking your normal putting stance, the toe of the putter is raised off the ground, then the lie of that putter is too upright. With the toe raised, you'll risk the chance of digging the heel into the green as you stroke your putt. Sure, Isao Aoki has made a comfortable living putting with the toe up. But he's the exception to the rule. We're looking for consistent results. You'll find them when the sole of the club lies flat against the ground in the address position.

The length of a putter, like the lie, can seriously affect your posture and your ability to make solid contact. If a putter is too long, it will

A putter with the correct lie angle will allow you to set up with your hands underneath your shoulders when the putter rests flat on the ground. If a putter is too upright, it will force your hands outside your shoulders. If it's too flat, it will force your hands inside your shoulders.

force you to stand farther away from the ball. As a result, your eyes will move to the inside of the target line and your hands will move outside your shoulder line. With both setup errors, you'll miss the putt to the right unless you make compensations. If a putter is too short for you, it will likely force you to crowd the ball or hunch over dramatically, causing your eyes to move outside the target line and your hands to move too far to the inside of the shoulder line. With these setup errors, you'll have the tendency to miss putts to the left — unless, of course, you make certain compensations.

Most putters are offered in shaft lengths that range from 32 to 37 inches. For players of average height and arm length, I recommend lengths of either 34 or 35 inches. Shorter players should use less length, taller players a little more. Ray Floyd, at 6'1", uses a 41-inch putter, which fits him perfectly because of his upright putting posture and shorter arm length. Jack Nicklaus, who stands 5'11", typically uses a putter only 33 inches long, since a short putter suits his recognizable crouch putting style.

If the lie angle is too upright, the toe will sit in the air and the heel will dig into the ground. Although some very successful Tour stars putt with the toe up, it can produce inconsistent results for most amateurs.

If the lie angle is too flat, the toe will dig and the heel will be off the ground.

Designs on Style

Once you become familiar with the lie and length values that match your setup posture, you're ready to embark on the second phase of putter selection: finding the appropriate style. This is the most difficult aspect of putter selection, since you must factor in the dynamics of your stroke and your preferences concerning feel, optics, and forgiveness.

Traditionally, a blade-style putter was recommended for players with wristy putting strokes. Players who preferred a pendulum-type stroke immediately opted for a heel-toe design. Golfers with inconsistent putting strokes who needed the ultimate in forgiveness were given mallets. These selections were made based on the weight-distribution properties of particular designs.

Putter experts have delineated four common putter designs. Although there are slight variations in each category, putters are available as end-shafted blades, center-shafted blades, heel-toe-weighted

A putter that is too long for you will force you to stand too erect, move your eyes inside the target line, and position your hands outside your shoulder line. Each of these setup errors puts into motion an inside takeaway.

A putter that's too short for you will force you to hunch over, move your eyes outside the target line, and position your hands inside your shoulder line. Each of these setup errors puts into motion an outside takeaway.

What About Long Putters?

Ten years ago, you would have raised a few eyebrows if you were to bring a long putter to your weekly match with your regular foursome. Today, it's a different story, because long putters have found their place as legitimate short-game tools.

Long putters can stretch up to 52 inches in length. Several Tour players putt with a long putter, the design parameters of which allow a golfer to putt while standing erect and with a split grip. The long putter can help players plagued by the yips or by an inconsistent stroke path, since it facilitates a pendulum-type stroke. Proponents of the long putter often claim that all they have to do is set the putter in motion on the takeaway and it does the rest. Bernhard Langer switched to a long putter to help battle his inconsistencies. So did Bruce Lietzke (shown above at the 1994 Phoenix Open), who has won his share of tournaments on the PGA Tour with a Leading Edge long putter.

PGA Tour player Rocco Mediate has also found success with a long putter. Mediate's affection for the long putter stems not from a need for a more reliable stroke, but to offset the pains and aches so many golfers experience when bending over to putt. For Mediate, such pain was too much to bear, especially after undergoing surgery in 1994 to repair a ruptured disk.

During his rehabilitation, Mediate discovered that the long putter placed less stress on his back. And it augmented the straight-back-straight-through stroke he had always employed. Selected out of necessity rather than convention, the long putter fueled Mediate's recovery. In 1996, he became the first player to birdie the last six holes at TPC at Sawgrass at The Players Championship. In 1999, he outlasted Tiger Woods to claim the Phoenix Open crown.

One of the best putters on the PGA Tour in 1999 was Scott McCarron. Scott uses a 48-inch long putter, slightly shorter than what Lietzke and Mediate use. This putter has paid untold dividends for McCarron, who gave up golf altogether after college to go into business. After four years, and after discovering the long putter, McCarron's passion again became golf. In 1999, McCarron ranked fifth in putts per green in regulation on the Tour.

The key to finding the appropriate length for a long putter is to match the length to your hip bend. Tilt from your hips as you would when taking your address position. Measure the distance from your breastbone to the point where your eyes make contact with the ground. That distance is the right length for your long putter.

models, and mallets. As you'll soon learn, each offers distinct performance characteristics that can add to or detract from your sense of feel and, ultimately, either augment or inhibit the success of your current putting style.

The End-Shafted Blade

If the persimmon, pear-shaped driver is the classic wood, then the end-shafted blade is the classic putter. Its design simply reflects its name: a flat blade with the shaft connection placed at the end, or heel, of the putter. The end-shafted blade's spartan design in no way denotes a lack of performance features. In fact, if a particular putter style had to be chosen as the one style to represent championship golf, it would be the end-shafted blade. Golfers with names like Jones, Palmer, and Crenshaw have taken home Green Jackets and Claret Jugs with these no-nonsense putting tools.

The key performance element of the end-shafted blade is what it doesn't have rather than what it does. Unlike more modern designs, which feature unique head shapes that distribute mass toward the heel, toe, face, or rear, the end-shafted blade lacks any specific weight

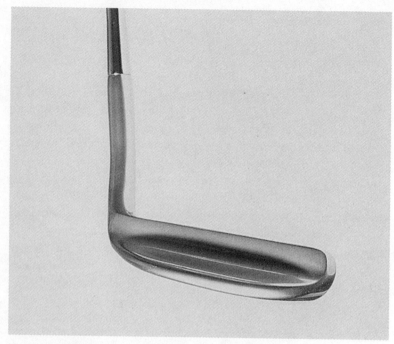

The famed Wilson 8802

distribution. Because of this, the end-shafted blade allows a golfer to better do with the putterhead what he wants to do with it—open the face on the takeaway, close the face at impact, etc. For many players, this freedom allows for a natural, "free-feeling" stroke. The next time you visit your local pro shop, pull a few end-shafted blades off the rack and putt a few balls. You'll notice how easy it is to control the putterhead. You'll also notice how easy it is to hit putts on the heel or toe. Putting with an end-shafted blade can be a rewarding experience, but it takes practice and there's less margin for error.

The end-shafted blade's uniform weight distribution, and the fact that the majority of these putters are forged from a solid block of carbon steel or similar soft material, provide for extraordinary feel and feedback to the hands. As a result, players who use end-shafted blades normally develop enhanced distance and speed control. The primary drawback of the end-shafted blade is its forgiveness, or lack thereof. In a recent robotic test, the end-shafted blade design, on putts hit toward the heel and toe, proved least effective compared to two other putter styles (mallet and heel-toe-weighted).

The World's Most Famous Putter

The most famous putter in the history of golf is "Calamity Jane," the putter used by the great Bobby Jones.

Jones began using Calamity Jane in 1920 after receiving it as a gift from Jim Maiden, a golf professional at the Nassau Country Club in Glen Cove, New York. Jim Maiden had names for most of his golf clubs. He dubbed his putter, which was forged by Scottish clubmaker Robert Condie of St. Andrews at the turn of the twentieth century, "Calamity Jane" after the straight-shooting wife of Wild Bill Hickok.

Maiden had given Jones his Calamity Jane to help the great amateur, who came to Nassau during a tremendous putting drought. Jones asked Maiden if he had any putters with which he could experiment. Maiden offered to let Jones try his Calamity Jane. Jones tried a dozen putts from all angles and made every one he looked at. "It's yours if you want it," Maiden told Jones. Jones accepted the gift and won Major championships in 1923, 1924, and 1925.

After a while, Jones noticed a defect in the sweet spot on the face of the putter. Apparently, Jones's caddies, who were eager to please the great champion, had worn a hole in the center of the putterface by cleaning Calamity Jane with emery cloths. Their diligence in keeping the great Bobby Jones's equipment in tip-top shape had damaged Calamity Jane beyond repair.

Spalding engineer J. Victor East made an exact copy of Calamity Jane in 1926 and dubbed it "Calamity Jane II." Jones won 10 of 13 Major championships with Calamity Jane II.

In 1948, Jones donated Calamity Jane I to Augusta National, where it's currently on display in the trophy room. Spalding began mass-producing the Calamity Jane putter with Jones's permission in 1932.

Classic end-shafted blades are rare in today's marketplace. You're more apt to find what can be called "modern" end-shafted blades, designed with offset hosels (which move the putterface behind the centerline of the shaft) and flanges jutting from the lower rear of the

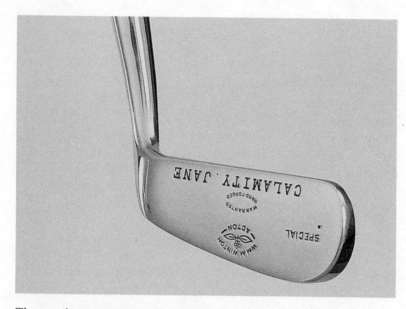

The most famous putter in golf, Calamity Jane can be yours thanks to Cleveland Golf, which offers an exact replica.

putterhead. These design improvements provide for a more forgiving putter. Regardless, the premium on control remains the telltale trait of the end-shafted blade.

The Center-Shafted Blade

Center-shafted blades differ from their end-shafted counterparts design-wise only in where the shaft connects to the head, which, as you might expect, is more toward the putter's center. Although the change is min-imal, moving the point of shaft insertion toward the center results in a completely different feel and overall weight distribution, and a perfor-mance that players such as Tom Kite, Steve Jones, and Corey Pavin—all U.S. Open champions—like. The most famous incarnation of the center-shafted blade is the Titleist Bulls Eye.

As is true of the end-shafted blade, the primary performance benefit of the center-shafted blade is that it gives the player freedom to move the putterhead as he or she wishes throughout the stroke. Many center-shafted blades feature extra mass toward the heel area, a design concept that facilitates a slight opening of the putterface on the takeaway and a slight closing through impact.

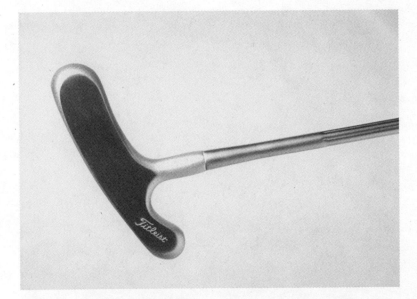

The Titleist Bulls Eye—the world's most popular center-shafted blade.

Heel-Toe-Weighted Models

Blade-style putters dominated the professional and amateur ranks for decades, until a small club-manufacturing company out of Scottsdale, Arizona, dropped the golf world on its ear by developing a putter drastically different in both design and performance. The heel-toe-weighted putter design—made popular by Karsten Solheim via his Ping Anser—finally provided golfers who couldn't hit the ball consistently in the center of the putterface with a workable alternative to blades.

Solheim engineered the Anser with a weight distribution that featured more mass positioned at the heel and toe than in the center of the putterhead. This resulted in a higher Moment of Inertia (MOI). For those of you who failed Physics 101 in college, MOI ranks an object's resistance to twisting. And that's exactly what Solheim's Anser and the gaggle of heel-toe-weighted putters that followed guarded against: putterhead twisting during impact.

Find a heel-toe-weighted putter and hit a few putts near the heel and toe. Although you won't get the full effect of the putter's ability to remain square on mishits, you should notice that, on the whole, these mishits roll surprisingly close to your intended line and near to your tar-

Ping's Scottsdale Anser: the original heel-toe putter

Heel-Toe Heaven

Forgiveness on off-center hits is an important design feature for amateur golfers, many of whom have difficulty in striking the ball in the center of the putterface. The loss of force and accuracy when a putt is hit toward the heel or toe will do more to raise your scores than any type of flaw you can work into your stroke. In a recent robotic test, putts hit on a flat putting surface as little as a quarter of an inch toward the heel and toe rolled as much as 12 inches to the left or right of the intended target and traveled 10 percent less than those struck in the middle of the putterface. The heel-toe-weighted design provided the tightest dispersion pattern on both heel and toe misses.

get. Repeat this exercise with an end-shafted blade and you'll discover far different results—specifically, a greater loss of accuracy and distance.

In addition to improving accuracy on mishits, the heel-toe weighted putter's weight distribution promotes a more pendulum-style putting motion in which the head remains perpendicular to the target line for the majority of the stroke.

Mallet

For many years, blade and heel-toe designs provided golfers with the tools to optimize either an inside-square-inside stroke or a pendulum-type motion. However, for many golfers, even these designs failed to provide the necessary forgiveness on putts hit off-center. This opened the door for the development of the mallet-style putter. Designed with a large, round head, the mallet was initially likened to a potato masher. And despite the fact that such notable players as Raymond Floyd and Dave Stockton approved of the mallet design, mallet putters failed to gain widespread acceptance until Nick Price used one to bag the 1994 British Open and another to fuel his historic hot streak in 1995.

It's interesting to note that the mallet, considered the most modern of the four styles discussed in this text, was used as early as 1904. Walter Travis, the first overpowering American amateur, put a strange-looking putter with a mallet-shaped head and center shaft placement into his bag for that year's British Amateur. Nicknamed the Schenectady for the town in which it was created, this new putter caused quite a stir as Travis holed a series of 20- to 35-foot putts in the final round against Edward Blackwell (who consistently outdrove Travis by 50 yards). After Travis claimed the Amateur title, the Royal & Ancient responded by deeming the design illegal. The ban continued until 1952.

Proponents of the mallet cite the confidence that the larger head and hitting area provide. Mallet enthusiasts also point to the placement of extra mass directly behind the sweet spot, which lessens the effect of mishitting a putt toward the heel or toe. In certain respects, the performance characteristics of mallet-style putters are similar to those of oversized drivers and irons, which have won over millions of amateur golfers with their ease of play.

Mallet putters are usually face-balanced, a design breakthrough originally patented by Ram Golf for use in its Zebra mallets. Face balancing incorporates a weighting strategy and shaft placement that

Never Compromise's Z|1 Alpha mallet

Putter Maintenance

If you're going to take care of any one piece of golf equipment in your bag, make sure it's your putter. The putter is a precision instrument and should be treated with the utmost care. Putterheads that are made from soft carbon steel, like Wilson's famed 8802 or many of Titleist's Scotty Cameron models, should be kept in a headcover not only between rounds, but also between holes during a round. Dings and chips on the putterface can definitely affect performance. Also, some models have special finishes that come off quite easily in damp conditions. When the finish comes off, the steel material underneath is left unprotected, and will rust quickly. A simple way to prevent this is to coat the putterhead with mineral oil (or common baby oil, which contains the same minerals) once every few months, and to make sure the putterhead is kept dry when not in use. It's also a good idea to occasionally clean the putter grip with liquid soap and warm water.

stabilizes the putterhead and keeps it square through impact. As such, mallets are considered the most forgiving of all putter styles.

Hybrids

Every putter on the market today can be classified as an end-shafted blade, center-shafted blade, heel-toe-weighted, or mallet, but many modern flatsticks borrow design features from each style. Some mallets are heel-toe-weighted; many heel-toe-weighted putters feature face balancing. Blades constructed with face inserts for greater perimeter weighting are increasing in popularity. Literally, there's a putter for every golfer.

The chart on page 74 outlines the basic design elements and performance characteristics of each of the four putter styles. Keep in mind, however, that one style of putter isn't necessarily better than another, and more modern design elements don't always indicate higher performance. As mentioned earlier, the best putter is one that fits your posture and hand position while giving you the best feel.

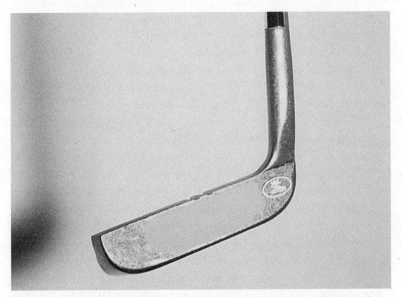

Hybrid putters such as the Bobby Grace by Cobra 2200 Softie, which combines insert technology with a classic blade design, blend the best of tradition and technology.

STYLE	PRIMARY DESIGN TRAIT	PRIMARY PERFORMANCE TRAIT	FORGIVENESS
End-Shafted Blade	Flat blade Weight distributed toward toe	Feel Feedback Control	Lowest
Center-Shafted Blade	Shaft insertion point toward center	Feel Feedback	Lowest
Heel-Toe-Weighted	Mass distributed toward heel and toe	Feel Stability	Higher
Mallet	Large, round head Face balancing More mass behind hitting area	Stability Forgiveness	Highest

Focus on Feel

How many times, when watching a putter advertisement on TV, have you heard the word "feel"? Manufacturers love the word "feel," as it brings to life the touch and skill so often associated with putting success. And to a certain extent it is. But it isn't as mystical as some people would have you believe. Nor are some golfers better able to tap into their sense of feel than others. The most important thing to remember about feel is that you'll never experience it unless you make solid ball–putterface contact. Feel is a product of consistently hitting putts in the center of the putterface. Hitting putts near the heel and toe will produce a certain feel, but it's not one you want to become familiar with.

Finding the right specs for your putter will strengthen your ability to hit the ball in the center of the putterface and, as a result, allow you to focus more on how a putter feels. That's why I'm presenting putter feel as the last step in the putter-selection process. Far too often, golfers use feel as the main determinant of which putters they purchase. What these golfers don't realize is that feel can come and go. You must make sure that a putter fits your posture and stroke first.

Nevertheless, the concept of feel is an important factor in finding the perfect putter. The problem is, feel is difficult to define, since it encompasses tactile, auditory, and visual sensations—subjective components that differ in intensity from one golfer to the next. There are several putter-design elements that contribute to the way a putter feels. Of these, optics, weighting, and materials are the most dominant. Simply varying these three can produce thousands of different putters.

Outlined below are five design options that can influence the feel of a given putter and, ultimately, how it performs.

Alignment Aids and Optics

Properly aligning your putterface to the intended target is crucial. Even if your speed and distance control are good, your chances of holing a given putt are slim if you're not aimed properly. Therefore, when purchasing a new putter, you have to find one that allows you to set up and align the head properly with consistency and confidence. To do this, you must discover which type of alignment schemes work best for you.

The most obvious alignment scheme takes the form of sight lines drawn on the top of the putterhead or the rear flange. These lines should be drawn parallel to the target line and perpendicular to the face of the club. Depending on their complexity, sight lines can go a long way in helping you ensure that your putterface is aligned properly to the target you intend to putt toward. One reason why mallets have grown in popularity is that their larger head size allows for longer sight lines and better reference to where the putterface is aimed. Think of your last three or four rounds. Did you miss most of your putts due to a lack of distance control? Or did your putts roll close enough to, but

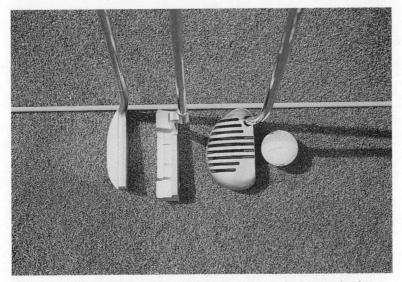

Alignment aids can give the golfer confidence at address. Aids can take the form of lines drawn on the putterhead, sight markings, and the shape of the putter itself.

slightly wide of, the cup? If you answered "yes" to the latter, then a mallet-style putter with alignment markings may greatly improve your performance on the green.

Alignment schemes can also take the form of the lines inherent in a putter's head shape. Ping's Anser putter, with its rectangular head, produces natural lines formed by the topline and leading edge that make it very easy to set the face perpendicularly to the target line. Most blades, which feature radiused heel and toe areas, lack this visual reference. The rounded head shape of some mallets can also confuse the eyes.

If you've had trouble finding a putter that helps you aim correctly, it could be that you're looking for gimmicks. Restart your search by focusing on putters with very clean toplines, straight leading edges, and an absence of rounded flanges, toe areas, and soles—especially if you've had some success in the past but are currently mired in a putting drought. Ping and Titleist have won over thousands of professional and amateur golfers by placing a premium on cleanliness and sharpness in their putter designs. These putters are said to have good optics—that is, they are designed to give the golfer confidence at address.

Materials

No other design option will impart more of an effect on how a putter feels than the choice of material from which the putter is constructed. Traditionally, putterheads were either cast or forged from stainless or carbon steel, both of which provide what many golfers refer to as a "solid" feel (on the continuum of softness, carbon steel is softer than most forms of stainless). An indication of a solid feel is an auditory "click" produced by ball–putterface contact. If you're a control-oriented putter, then you've typically relied on this click as feedback to the senses to better regulate the distance and speed of your putts.

Today, putter manufacturers leave no element in the periodic table unturned. Some of the many materials used in putter design are aluminum, bronze, nickel, brass, titanium, and copper, as well as alloys composed of several different metals. It can be argued that the use of metals other than steel has been fueled by the recent trend toward softer-feeling putters. This may be true, but most experienced putter designers will tell you that the use of one material over another has more to do with weighting than feel. Aluminum, for example, is much lighter than stainless steel and, therefore, can be used to construct either a lightweight putter or a standard-weight putter with a larger head size. Lighter materials can be used in combination with heavier ones to create extreme heel-toe weighting or to place extra mass behind the sweet spot.

Inserts

When Nick Faldo claimed the 1996 Masters using an Odyssey Dual Force Rossie, the putter industry was changed forever, as it marked the first time a Major championship was won with an insert putter. All weekend long, TV viewers got a bird's-eye view of Faldo holing putts left and right with the funny-looking mallet with the shiny black putter-face—a design that helped propel Odyssey to the top of the putting charts in terms of use on the professional tours. Amateurs wanted in on the action, too, and soon it seemed that every 2-, 10-, and 20-handicapper was putting with an Odyssey or one of the many other putters designed with polymer-based face inserts, giving credence to the phrase "What wins on Sunday sells on Monday."

The effect of face inserts on putting is twofold. First, it creates greater perimeter weighting, since the material the face insert displaces is much heavier than the insert itself. And that's a good thing for players who have difficulty striking the ball in the center of the clubface consistently. (Never Compromise's family of flatsticks features face inserts that form the entire midsection of the putterhead, pushing the heel-toe weight-distribution envelope to the extreme.) Second, face inserts are noticeably softer than the majority of metals traditionally used in putter construction. Hence, they increase dwell time, or the period the ball remains in contact with the putterface. This is an important feature of face inserts, since increased dwell time increases the amount of feedback to the body and mind. As such, inserts can accelerate a player's development in terms of distance and speed control.

Additionally, face inserts can benefit players who typically use harder, two-piece balls. These ball types, which can help less-skilled players negate the effects of a slice or hook swing, have traditionally been labeled as poor tools for the touch and control that putting requires. But the softer face of an insert putter can relay proper feel despite the ball's hardness.

Opponents of face inserts note that the softer material forces a more aggressive stroke in order to putt a ball the same distance as a ball rolled with a harder putterface. This is simply not the case, since the force of

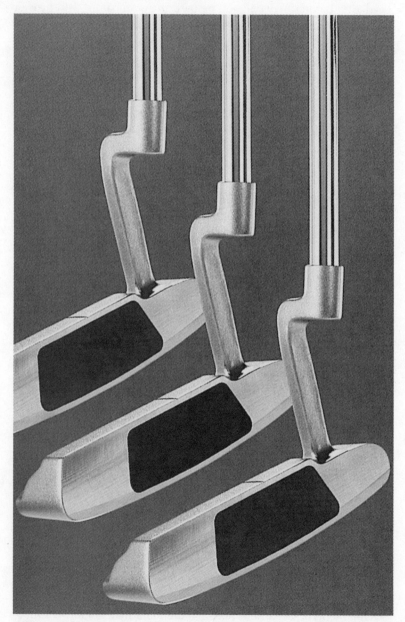

Odyssey Golf, and its patented Stronomic face material, ushered in the face-insert age.

Choosing the Best Ball

Can the type of golf ball with which you typically play make a difference in your putting? According to a recent robotic test, the answer is "Yes!"

Basically, there are three ball-construction types: two-piece distance, three-piece wound, and multilayer. Traditional two-piece balls have a large, solid core and a hard, durable outer cover. These design elements combine to produce extra distance off full-swing shots. Three-piece golf balls are typically composed of a smaller, liquid-filled rubber center, a wound midsection, and a thin, soft cover. These balls are softer than two-piece balls, don't fly as far, and tend to spin at higher rates. Multilayer balls, a design made famous by Top-Flite's Strata, blend distance and durability with a softer feel and more spin.

The three-piece wound ball has been the consistent favorite of Tour pros, since players of such caliber normally do not require the extra distance that a two-piece ball can provide. Instead, advanced players emphasize feel, especially on delicate pitch shots and, of course, all putts.

While the feel benefits of three-piece balls can never be disputed, the robotic test showed that on putts hit in the center of the putterface, the three-piece design was the least consistent in terms of distance. In fact, putt distances ranged from a low of 20.5 feet to 23.5 feet with the same stroke length and force. The discrepancy in distances was attributed to the three-piece construction process, which contains the largest number of variables and greatest room for inconsistency.

Surprisingly, the two-piece design showed a tighter dispersion pattern and rolled noticeably farther than the three-piece models. The multilayer model proved even more impressive. In fact, the multilayer balls all rolled within a foot of each other.

With its tighter dispersion patterns and enhanced feel, the multilayer design, according to many experts, represents the future of golf ball construction.

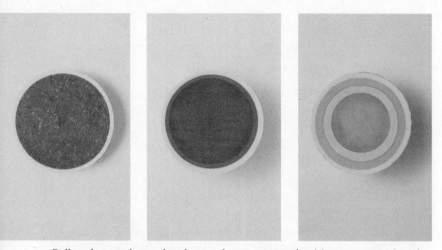

Balls today are designed with two, three, or upwards of four pieces, each with inherent feel and distance qualities.

a standard putting stroke isn't great enough to compress a golf ball. Face inserts are all about feel and feedback.

If you're familiar with the newest putter models, you know that soft resins and plastics dominate the face insert segment of the market. However, a number of manufacturers are experimenting with inserts made from more traditional materials, such as copper, as well as from metal alloys. While these materials are definitely harder than the polymers used in other inserts, they provide a feel that promotes ample softness and increases the amount of information transferred to the hands.

The most important thing to remember about inserts is that they're a personal preference. Before you buy a putter with or without a face insert, decide which provides the most sensation to your hands.

Face Balancing

Typically, blade-style and heel-toe-weighted putters are toe-balanced. This means that they're designed with a particular weight distribution and shaft connection such that, if you held the putter across your finger just a few inches above the hosel, the toe would point straight down. As stated earlier, this type of balancing facilitates an inside-square-inside putting stroke. Some putters are fully toe-balanced, meaning the toe will point straight down if you held the putter in the manner outlined above. Others will point down at an angle of 80 degrees, some at

40 degrees, and others at 20 degrees. The exact amount of "face-down angle" relates to how easily a golfer can manipulate the position of the putterhead when stroking a putt.

What makes the mallet design unique is that most feature face balancing. If you hold a face-balanced putter across your finger, the toe won't drop toward the ground. Rather, in what may appear to be sheer defiance of gravity, the face will point directly skyward. What this design breakthrough means to the golfer is that the clubhead will tend to stay square to the target line throughout the stroke. So, if you happen to putt with a vertical, straight-back and straight-through stroke, you'll probably do best with a face-balanced putter. If you get the most successful results putting on an inside-square-inside stroke, you'll want to pick something else.

Although face balancing is typically associated with the mallet design, more and more manufacturers are offering face-balanced, heel-toe-weighted putters. Such a design should benefit players who tend to putt with a pendulum stroke but who are more comfortable with the optics and feel of the heel-toe design.

Putters come with varying "face down" angles. Putters that are face-balanced feature a weight distribution and shaft geometry that facilitates keeping the putterface square during the putting stroke.

Offset Hosels

While I stand behind my belief that putting styles defy conformity, I will state that most successful putters putt with their hands positioned at least even or slightly ahead of the putterhead. Players whose wrists break down during the stroke or who allow the putterhead to race ahead of the hands through the impact zone, in my opinion, will have a difficult time realizing consistent results. A design option that helps the hands maintain their proper position during the stroke is the offset hosel.

An offset hosel moves the putterface behind the centerline of the shaft. If you take your stance and grip with a putter with an offset hosel, you'll find that your hands are automatically positioned ahead of the ball before you even begin your motion. The offset can take the form of either a bend in the shaft or a 90-degree crook in the hosel. Either way, offset hosels place the hands in an ideal position to begin the putting stroke and keeps them there as the putterhead moves through impact.

If you've played with a non-offset hosel for any length of time and have experienced scuffing (or turf drag), you might develop a firmer

Offset hosels come in the form of crooks and double-bend shafts. An offset hosel puts the hands in the desired forward position without the golfers having to forward-press, a move that can potentially subtract loft from the putterface.

stroke if you switch to a putter with an offset hosel. Likewise if you notice your ball bouncing as it makes its way toward the target, which is caused by delofting the clubface through too much forward pressing with the hands. An offset hosel helps a player strike the putt with the exact loft that's built into the putterface by placing the hands forward without your having to forward-press.

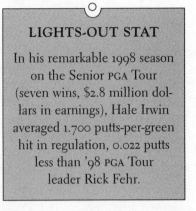

LIGHTS-OUT STAT

In his remarkable 1998 season on the Senior PGA Tour (seven wins, $2.8 million dollars in earnings), Hale Irwin averaged 1.700 putts-per-green hit in regulation, 0.022 putts less than '98 PGA Tour leader Rick Fehr.

An additional asset of offset hosels is that they usually move the shaft out of your sight line when you look down at the putterhead at address. An uncluttered view will augment your ability to align the putterhead perpendicularly to the target line. As I mentioned earlier, clean lines promote better alignment.

A caveat to keep in mind concerning offset hosels is that they typically force a golfer to align to the right. The reason is that offset hosels give the appearance that the head is pointing left of square. Therefore, golfers will automatically adjust their alignment to the right to compensate for what they think is a "closed" putterface. This can cause severe problems if you typically align right of your target. (Keep in mind that most golfers usually align to the left or right of where they think they're aimed. Very few golfers have the ability to align the putterhead perfectly straight.) If you typically aim right, and adjust to the right due to the offset hosel, you'll find your putts traveling severely off-line. PGA Tour player Robert Gamez, with whom I've had the privilege of working, typically aligns left of where he thinks he's aimed. The offset hosel helps him to adjust his setup to the right. In this example, the offset allows him to set up square to the target with consistency.

Can Grips Make a Difference?

When purchasing a new putter, many amateurs focus too much on the head. There's nothing wrong with this, unless you forget about inspecting the grip. Don't be content to play with the grip that comes standard with a given putter. Realize that there are too many different grip options not to do a little experimenting.

Natural leather used to be the overwhelming choice of control-oriented putters. Recently, manufacturers have developed synthetic rubber compounds that combine the feel of leather with added durability.

A more important issue is size. Grips are available in four standard sizes, and each can be built up with tape to provide an infinite number of dimensions. As a general rule, the less handsy your stroke, the larger the grip should be. A larger grip helps to inactivate the hands, a crucial component of the popular one-piece pendulum stroke. The next time you're browsing through the putter rack, try an oversized grip. Many amateur and professional golfers alike have found that larger grips help to reduce unwanted wrist and hand action in their strokes. Buyer beware: a larger, heavier grip can reduce your putter's swing weight, which can disrupt your natural tempo and rhythm.

In regard to grip shape, there are two options. One is the paddle-style grip, which features a wide flat part for the placement of the thumbs. A paddle-style grip is considered conducive to a one-piece stroke where the hands play a minor role. The other is a pistol grip, characterized by a protruding section on the back of the handle, which provides for more control. These grips get their name from the feeling the hands receive when holding a putter with this type of handle, similar to gripping a pistol.

Whatever grip you choose, pay particular attention to the top portion of the handle. The flat, top part can be used as a secondary, or even primary, alignment feature. By guaranteeing that the flat part angles directly toward the ball, you'll guarantee that the putterface is neutral and not pointing to the left or right.

Lessons in Loft

Most weekend players aren't aware that putters are constructed with varying degrees of loft. Although the exact amount of loft is small compared to the loft of an iron or wedge, it can seriously affect your performance on the green.

You'll find that most putters come with a loft of four degrees. However, if you were to pool every putter on the market today, you'd find that the range of putter loft starts at zero and runs as high as 8 degrees. Generally, the lower the amount of loft, the quicker the ball will get rolling end over end after it's struck.

When deciding what amount of loft is right for your putter, it's important to take into account the type of greens on which you play the majority of your rounds. If you play on smooth, fast greens, opt for less loft, since you want the ball to start rolling on the surface earlier than later. If most of your rounds are played on public courses, where the greens are typically bumpy or are mowed infrequently, opt for a putter that features more loft. With a more-lofted putter, the ball will actually rise off the putting surface before it starts rolling toward the target, lessening the effect of a green's inconsistency.

Another thing to keep in mind when deciding the appropriate loft for your putter is whether or not you press your hands forward before you begin your stroke. When you forward-press, you actually deloft the putterface. Therefore, if you purchase a putter with only 2 degrees of loft, and you forward-press, you'll risk the chance of stroking the ball downward into the turf (which will invariably cause the ball to jump off your intended target line). I recommend a putter with at least 5 degrees of loft if you typically forward-press.

Roll Faces

It's not always certain that you'll strike the ball with the exact amount of loft built into your putterface. Inconsistencies in your stroke and setup can make it easy to add or subtract loft at impact, affecting your distance control. If you feel that your stroke produces varying degrees of "dynamic" loft, then you might want to give the TD series of putters from TearDrop Golf a committed try.

All of TearDrop's putters feature what the company calls "Roll-Face" technology. What this means is that the putterface is slightly curved, giving the putter a dynamic loft of 4 degrees. According to Teardrop, the concave curve of the putterhead produces a consistent loft angle, regardless of where your hands are at impact. To a degree, it doesn't matter if you strike the ball on the upswing or downswing—you'll always make contact with the same amount of loft. In this respect alone, Roll-Face technology can benefit your ability to control the distance you hit your putts.

Cost

What price perfection? When it comes to putters, the sky appears to be the limit, especially with the advent of multimaterial designs, proprietary face inserts, and graphite shafts. These high-performance features can come with a wallet-depleting price tag. In fact, some of the more technologically advanced putters retail for hundreds of dollars. Hand

---

BEN CRENSHAW—A LIGHTS-OUT PUTTER

With three NCAA titles and 19 Tour wins, two-time Masters champion Ben Crenshaw has always been considered one of the purest putters in the game of golf. With a deliberate, but smooth, inside-square-inside stroke—like a door opening and closing—Crenshaw canned numerous important putts throughout his career, including a 60-foot birdie at the '84 Masters that led to his first Green Jacket. Eleven years later, at the '95 Masters, Crenshaw made an equally important—though less lengthy—10-foot birdie putt on the 71st hole to beat Davis Love III by one stroke and earn his second Masters victory.

According to "Gentle Ben," the key to his putting success has been the simplicity of his philosophy and technique, an uncomplicated approach that helped him to victory in his very first event as a professional (the 1973 Texas Open). Using his trusted Wilson 8802 end-shafted putter (and a similar model made by Cleveland later in his career), Crenshaw concentrates on being comfortable and relaxed over the ball, and maintaining an even tempo from backstroke to finish. Above all, Crenshaw focuses on staying down through the putt. "If you stay down," he says, "you'll always give yourself a chance."

---

craftsmanship also demands a premium, although these putters tend to be more consistent than cast models.

When shopping for a new putter, the best advice is to stick to your budget. If you have $300 to spend, go for it. You'll probably find a great putter. If your budget is only $150, there's no need to worry. In fact, the majority of putters used on the professional tours fall into this price category. If you have less than $80 to spend, accept the fact that you probably won't be playing with the best the golf industry has to offer, unless you opt for a used putter.

A final thought for budgeting for a new putter: How much money have you invested in reaching the green? Four hundred dollars for a driver? One thousand dollars for your irons and wedges? Count it up. These clubs are used for nearly half of your shots on the course. You use the putter for the other half. What's its worth? The point is, don't be afraid to spend a little money on the one club that will do more to lower your scores than any other in the bag.

5

Perfect Practice Makes Perfect

The harder I practice, the luckier I get.
—*Gary Player*

If you've played golf for any length of time, it's likely that you understand the importance of putting as it relates to your scores. In a nutshell, putts add up. As I stated earlier, if you miss a green, you can always chip it close and salvage a par. But miss a putt, and the stroke is gone forever.

In a perfectly played round on a typical golf course, one in which you hit every green in regulation and make every putt, you'll post a 54 with 18 putts. In this scenario, putting accounts for 33 percent of the total number of strokes. A good round on the PGA Tour, one in which a player hits 75 percent of the greens and needs only 27 putts, typically results in a score of around 67 or 68. In this scenario, putting accounts for roughly 35 percent of the total number of strokes.

Thirty-five percent—and this from the best players in the world at the top of their games. It makes sense, then, that at least 35 percent of their practice time should be devoted to putting. Now, think about your game. If you're a typical weekend player, you shoot in the low 90s and need anywhere from 30 to 36 putts to complete your round. At this level, putting accounts for up to 40 percent of your score. After spending hundreds of hours at professional tournament venues, especially on practice days, I know for a fact that PGA Tour players devote ample time to practicing their putting. I also know that amateurs rarely come close to putting in the time necessary to become a consistently good putter—certainly not 40 percent. When most amateurs practice, the putter is usually the last club to be pulled from the bag, if it's pulled at all. The 7-iron and driver are what usually dominate the practice session.

If this is typical of you, ask yourself this question: how often do you hit your driver during a round? At most, you'll need it 14 times, probably less. On the other hand, you'll need your putter anywhere from 24 to 36 times. Therefore, you should practice your putting twice as much as you practice your long game.

I understand that these facts are difficult to swallow, especially if you struggle with your driver and it often leaves you with difficult second shots. A commitment to putting practice takes self-discipline. I want you to practice your full swing. After all, if you can't get off the tee, your scores will always be higher than you'd like. But, as I said earlier, a good putting stroke can truly help your scores from ballooning on your off

---

Putt for Dough

In the high-stakes world of professional golf, even one more missed putt per round can throw a player back to the middle of the pack. Listed below are pros who have shown marked improvement in their putting (indicated by the putts-per-green statistic kept by the PGA Tour) between 1996 and 1998. As you can see, a small improvement in the ability to roll the ball into the hole more consistently can pay huge dividends. In fact, the players on this list averaged 205 percent more in earnings in 1998 than in 1996.

As a group, these players decreased their putting average by 0.035 putts per green. Do some math and you'll find that this improvement statistically dropped approximately two strokes from a typical four-day tournament score. A decrease in putting average also appears to have bettered these players' birdie-per-round average (the Birdie Differential column compares the 1996 birdie average to the 1998 birdie average). A birdie differential of +0.5, for example, indicates that a player averaged two more birdies per tournament in 1998 than in 1996.

Golfers confused by the recent demise of such notable stars as Corey Pavin and Nick Faldo may find the answers by looking into these players' putting stats. Pavin dropped 79 spots in the

days. A made putt can make up for an errant drive, or even a penalty stroke. Good scores begin and end with good putting. So you need to alter your practice approach and give your putting the attention it deserves.

In instructing my students on how to properly practice, I always ask them to start at the hole and work backward. That is, begin the practice session on the putting green, then work through chips, pitches, and other greenside shots before moving on to short irons, long irons, and, finally, the driver. The benefits of this type of arrangement are three-fold. First, you'll devote more practice time to your putting stroke. Second, practicing putting will force you to think more about your whole game than simply trying to hit the ball as straight and as far as you possibly can. Third, saving the full swing for last will ensure that

putting statistic between 1996 and '98. Faldo carded birdie on seven fewer holes per tournament in '98 compared to his '96 average.

PLAYER	'96 MONEY	'96 PUTTING AVERAGE (RANK)	'98 MONEY	'98 PUTTING AVERAGE (RANK)	BIRDIE DIFFERENTIAL
Bob Estes	$123,100	1.817 (158)	$ 987,930	1.747 (12)	+0.77
Andrew Magee	$332,504	1.786 (73)	$ 964,302	1.761 (29)	+0.24
Brandel Chamblee	$233,265	1.796 (105)	$ 755,936	1.771 (51)	+0.46
Chris Perry	$184,171	1.789 (83)	$ 730,171	1.746 (10)	+0.29
Billy Andrade	$433,157	1.775 (47)	$ 705,434	1.747 (12)	+0.10
Ted Tryba	$162,994	1.804 (125)	$ 421,786	1.780 (73)	+0.12
David Duval	$977,079	1.776 (49)	$2,591,031	1.732 (5)	+0.36
Jim Furyk	$814,334	1.769 (37)	$2,054,334	1.745 (9)	+0.20
Hal Sutton	$193,723	1.796 (105)	$1,838,740	1.772 (55)	+0.12
John Huston	$506,173	1.765 (29)	$1,554,110	1.730 (4)	+0.16
Bob Tway	$529,456	1.793 (97)	$1,073,447	1.749 (17)	+0.68
Corey Pavin	$851,320	1.768 (34)	$168,485	1.793 (113)	−0.48
Nick Faldo	$942,621	1.748 (8)	$150,703	1.838 (182)	−1.17

you're properly warmed up and that your timing is set for the demands the driver swing requires.

Practice Types

There are two types of putting practice: fundamental practice and confidence practice. In the former practice, the focus is on your mechanics and your stroke. In the latter, the focus is on building trust in your stroke to clear your mind of doubt and allow it to focus on your goals.

Fundamental practice should always come before confidence practice. After all, if you want to build trust in your fundamentals, you have to have a good setup and stroke. You don't want to build confidence in a stroke that produces fair results at best. As I stated earlier, perfecting the fundamentals of putting takes practice. Your fundamental practice sessions provide the time for you to do just that.

Fundamental Practice

Putting practice, for many, can be a boring, monotonous task, which explains why so many weekend players don't devote enough practice time to their putting strokes. The self-discipline of a Phil Mickelson, who often practices nothing but three-footers a hundred at a time, is rare. That's why I provide my students with a number of drills and games to perform on the practice green. Drills are great because they give structure to a practice session. Plus, it's a lot easier to remain focused during a 10-minute drill than it is to remain focused while mindlessly rolling putts.

The following drills will help you perfect your setup and stroke during your fundamental practice sessions. You don't have to perform all of them during each and every practice session. But at the very least, practice your setup every time you practice your putting. Reserve the first 10 minutes of every practice session for your setup fundamentals. Then vary the drills according to what facets of your putting need the most work.

Practicing the Setup

To properly practice your setup, you'll need a visual reference. That's why I like to run a chalk line on the putting green. The chalk line provides a reference as to what your eyes perceive as "straight" as you address your putt. As I mentioned earlier, getting a straight-line

With your chalk line or string in place, verify that the elements of your setup are correct. Pay special attention to your shoulders, which should be aligned parallel to the target line.

perspective is difficult even for the most advanced golfers. You'll need a chalk line to verify that you're addressing the ball correctly.

In lieu of a chalk line, you can also use a string tied to two pencils. Make sure the string is high enough so that your putter can move easily underneath it.

With your visual reference in place (either the chalk line or the string), address a golf ball. Now, before you go any further, take inventory of your setup and check these key requirements:

- Putterface aligned perpendicularly to the line
- Shoulders aligned parallel to the line
- Eyes positioned directly over the line
- Hands hanging directly beneath your shoulders
- Weight evenly balanced over lower body

As we saw in Chapter 2, these five requirements can make or break your putting stroke. As you stand over the chalk line, be very critical of your setup in regard to these five positions. I want you to nail down these positions so that you can walk into your setup every time and achieve perfection without having to think about it. Your body is a very dynamic entity. As such, it's very easy to fall in and out of a perfect setup. That's why the pros spend so much time practicing it.

I recommend that you perform the chalk line drill at least once a week. You'll find that, as time passes, the chalk line drill will serve more to simply verify that your setup is intact, rather than to help you move your body to satisfy the five requirements. Practicing your setup is like going to the dentist: Most of the time it's only a checkup. Miss a few appointments, however, and you'll run into some trouble.

Practicing the Stroke
The setup drill with the chalk line should take no more than five to 10 minutes. Once you're satisfied with your setup, you can use the chalk line (or string) to practice your basic stroke mechanics.

Missed putts are the result of either not stroking the ball the appropriate distance, not hitting the putt along the intended line, or a combination of both. Not hitting the putt along the intended line wields the greatest influence, especially on shorter putts. (On longer putts, distance and direction will have equal influence.) After all, you can hit the ball slightly too far or slightly too little and still give the putt a good chance

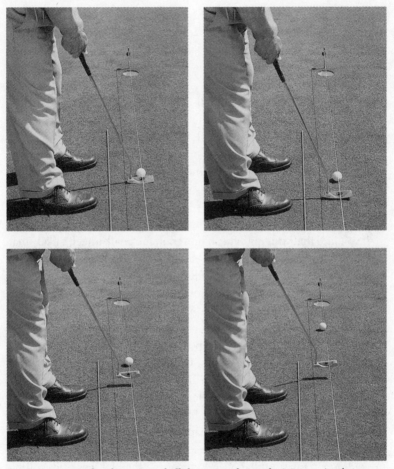

Practice your stroke along your chalk line or underneath a string. Analyze your motion with two keys in mind. One: on shorter putts, the putterhead travels along the target line (i.e., the chalk line or the string) from takeaway to finish. Two: the putterhead remains low to the ground (don't allow the putterhead to graze the string during any part of the stroke).

to fall into the hole, depending on the slope. Err on the direction side, however, and you usually have no chance of success whatsoever.

What forces players to mishit their putts? The answer is by moving the putterhead off-line during the stroke or by adding or subtracting loft from the putterface. If you take the putterhead outside or inside the target line on the backstroke, you'll likely cut across or push the ball on the forward stroke. If you swing the putterhead too high into the air, you'll change your putter's loft at impact, making it difficult to putt a good roll on the ball. The most reliable stroke, again, is one in which the putterhead travels along the target line and as low to the ground as possible during the stroke.

You can now see how the chalk line can help you ingrain such a stroke. Assume your stance over the chalk line with the correct setup, and start making practice strokes. Use the chalk line as a reference to where your putterhead moves to on the backstroke and the forward stroke. Try to keep the putterhead moving directly on the line throughout your motion. I like to have my students stop their strokes at the end of the backstroke and analyze their putterhead position from there; likewise for the follow-through.

If you find that your putterhead moves off the chalk line, it's likely that you're manipulating the clubhead with your hands or that you've built up too much tension in your arms. Remember, you want your hands to play a minor role in the putting stroke. Your arms are what should dictate your putting motion. Focus on your big muscles, specifically your forearms and shoulders, and work on adopting a lighter grip pressure.

Another thing to look for when performing this drill is that your putterhead remains low to the ground. If you let your arms dominate, you should have no problem accomplishing this. If, however, your hands or shoulders are too active, your putterhead will rise on the backstroke, making it difficult to stroke the ball on its equator with the center of your putterface. What will likely happen is that you'll contact the ball either on a slightly ascending or descending arc, causing it to jump off the putterface uncontrollably and increasing the chances of its rolling off your intended line.

Notice how I've yet to ask you to actually putt a golf ball. That's perfectly okay, because players, when practicing, typically focus too much of their attention on results rather than on the specifics of their setup or swing. Plus, you don't necessarily need a ball to check your setup or stroke—the chalk line will tell the story in full.

Practicing Tempo and Distance Control

A smooth tempo is crucial to controlling the speed of your putts and, as a result, the distance they travel. It's impossible to stroke the ball consistently if you yank the putterhead back and jab at the ball coming through. The idea is to take the same amount of time in your backstroke as you do in your forward stroke. It doesn't matter how long a putt is—your stroke should feel equal going back and through.

One of the best ways to work on your putting tempo is with a metronome, which sets a perfect rhythm at whatever speed you desire with a clicking sound as it rocks back and forth. Many players on the Tour practice with a metronome before every practice session, matching the timing of their stroke with the click of the metronome back and through, back and through. I recommend you get hold of a metronome and use it often to practice your rhythm and tempo. Not only will it augment the pace of your stroke, but it will help you build a more fluid putting motion.

The metronome can also be used to hone your distance control, specifically by helping you match stroke length with how far you want the ball to travel. Remember, you want a constant tempo, whether the putt is three feet or 30 feet. The only variable is how far you take the putterhead back and through.

Find a nice, flat section on the practice green and place tees in the ground at five-foot intervals from the cup to 30 feet out. Set your metronome and practice putts at each length. Concentrate on your tempo by matching the timing of your stroke with the click of the

Practice putts from different lengths to help you match backstroke lengths with how far you want the ball to travel.

metronome. As you move from one distance to the next, take stock of how far back you need to take your putter in order to roll the ball the appropriate length. Make a mental note of specific stroke lengths so you can refer back to them when faced with similar-length putts on the course. Remember, no matter how long your stroke is, it must always move in time with the tempo set by the metronome.

There are many other putting drills you can perform, but, in my opinion, executing these three will train you in each crucial element of putting: setup, stroke, tempo, and distance control.

However, if your goal is to truly become a lights-out putter, you'll need to augment your practice time with several other drills and games. What's different about these drills from the ones listed above is that they're result-based—you'll want to try to make every putt you practice. The best thing about these drills is that they're challenging and, to a certain degree, a lot of fun, which is a good thing because players rarely associate putting practice with a good time.

It's also not a bad idea to perform these drills with a friend. Each one can be set up as a kind of game. Make a friendly wager and challenge one of your golfing buddies to a putting contest using one of the drills. The added pressure of competition in practice will help you handle pressure on the course. Also, anything that can make practice appear like anything other than practice will help you to train more and for a longer period of time.

Drill One: 50-Point Putting Game

Recently, I learned a great putting game from teaching professional Ron Biddleman. I like the 50-Point Putting Game because not only does it reward success, but it enhances a golfer's distance control, as well.

Basically, points are awarded for made putts and subtracted for misses. Putts that finish within a "safety zone," roughly 18 inches behind the cup, are awarded zero points. The fact that the safety zone is beyond the hole demands that you at least try to get the ball all the way to the cup. That's a key element to lights-out putting: you have to give every putt a chance.

The game begins three feet (one pace) from the hole. Putt one ball from here. A make is worth 1 point, a miss, −3. Proceed to nine feet (three paces), and increase the point value to 2 (−1 for a miss). Next, 15 feet, or five paces (3 points, −1 point), then finally 21 feet, or seven paces (4 points, −1 point). If you sink every putt, you get 10 points. Miss

50-POINT PUTTING GAME

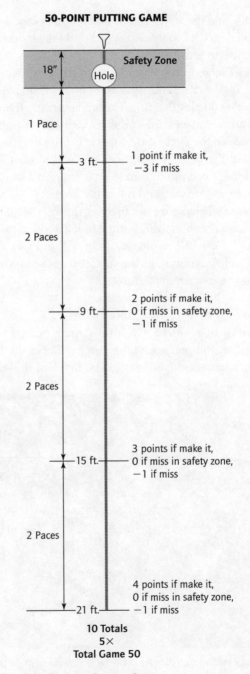

The setup and rules of the 50-Point Putting Game

every putt—and the safety zone—and it's –6 points. After you attempt the 21-footer, go back to three feet and start the process again until you complete five rounds.

A perfect score in the 50-Point Putting Game is 50. Tour pros average in the high teens, while most of my amateur students average in the low teens. As you play the game over and over, you'll find that your best scores result not necessarily from making lots of putts but from not missing outside the safety zone, especially from the longer putt lengths. Your skill in the 50-Point Putting Game will ultimately pay dividends on the course, since you'll learn to leave yourself with easy second putts while giving your first a good roll at the hole.

For an added challenge, set up the game on a sloping section of the green. Create uphill, downhill, right-to-left and left-to-right versions of the game. Your score on sloping putts will tell you a lot about your strengths and weaknesses, giving you feedback as to what types of putts you should be practicing the most.

Drill Two: Third of the Hole
Here's a drill that will help you on sloping putts. First, find a good uphill putt on the practice putting green. Cover the low third of the hole with a scorecard (you can secure the card to the ground with a

Cover the low third of the hole to develop the skill required to die the ball on downhill putts, charge uphill putts, and drop into the high side of the hole on breaking putts.

couple of tees). The idea is that uphill putts need to hit the back of the hole. If you putt your ball with too weak a stroke, it won't get past the card. That's the same as a miss. On downhill putts, cover the back half of the hole with the scorecard. With the card over the back half of the hole, you'll learn how to die downhill putts over the front of the cup. I'm sure you've hit a few downhill putts over the years that were struck too hard, hit the back of the hole, and popped out.

The Third of the Hole drill works with left-to-right and right-to-left breaking putts, as well. On a breaking putt, cover the low side of the hole. This will help you narrow your focus on the high side of the hole, which is where you want all of your breaking putts to pour into.

Drill Three: Through the Gate

Another drill to better your stroke on breaking putts is Through the Gate. Find a curving, right-to-left breaking putt on the practice putting green. Place two tees roughly two inches away from each other at a 45-degree angle one inch from the high side of the hole. The objective is to hole the putt through the gate. If you play too little break, or overpower the break with a forceful stroke, the ball will strike the front tee and rebound away from the cup. Only the most accurately struck putt and a perfect read will allow the ball to pass through the gate and into the hole.

An important thing to remember is that these drills make up your fundamental practice. They're for nonplaying days only, or for your postround practice time. Fundamental practice is exactly that: practicing your fundamentals. A 100-yard sprinter wouldn't run his or her rota of practice sprints right before a big race. Nor should you work on your mechanics before a round. Fundamental practice hones your mechanics so that you can use them instinctively during a round. If you practice mechanics before you play, you'll invariably wind up practicing them as you play. And that's a recipe for disaster. Now, it's important to hit the practice green before you tee off, but that's not training, that's warming up—or, as I like to refer to it, confidence practice.

Confidence Practice

Good putting is like a good marriage: You need trust and commitment—a trust in your abilities and a commitment to the line that you've chosen to putt along. So far, we've talked about training your setup, training

Practicing the Through the Gate drill will help you to understand that the front of the hole moves to the line of the putt. This drill also emphasizes the correct speed on breaking putts.

your stroke, and training your distance control. Now it's time to learn how to trust your setup, trust your stroke, and trust your ability to control the distance of your putts. The best time to build trust in your stroke is just prior to your play. If you can learn to use your warm-up time before a round as a trust-building session, you'll find your putting mechanics on automatic pilot as you traverse the course. That's when you'll have the best chance to shoot lower scores.

LIGHTS-OUT STAT

Greg Norman's 68.81 stroke average in 1994 landed him that year's Vardon Trophy, and is the lowest adjusted average to date. During the '94 season, Norman averaged 1.747 putts per green in regulation, the lowest average of his notable career.

Usually, golfers leave themselves with only 10 to 15 minutes or so to warm up before they play. If this is typical of you, I recommend that you use at least five minutes building trust in your putting stroke. For those of you who generally opt to spend all of your preround practice time at the range, remember: five minutes on the practice tee will loosen you up, but five minutes on the practice green will lower your scores.

Plus, you'll need to experience the putting-surface conditions of the course you're about to play. You never want to play a course half-blinded by not knowing the speed, grain, and turf type of the putting greens. I don't care how many different courses you've played, fairway grass is fairway grass and rough is rough. Greens are a different animal altogether. An unfamiliar green can wreak havoc on your round if you're not prepared. You've got to get a feel for the greens each and every time you play.

Ideally, you should give yourself at least 45 minutes to warm up. This provides enough time to warm up your putting, practice your pitches and chips, and figure out what to expect from your full swing on any given day. Regardless, no matter how much in advance of your scheduled tee time you arrive at the course, hit the putting green first to build trust in your stroke.

Trusting Your Preputt Routine

Owning a preputt routine that you can consistently count on is paramount for success. In my many conversations with Tour pros, they tell me that when they're feeling the pressure, it's usually their preputt routine that gets them through, especially on the putting green, where the tension and pressure are at their greatest.

Therefore, the first part of your confidence practice is to go through your preshot routine. Lay a ball down on the practice putting green, and act as if it's the last putt on the 18th green and you need to sink it for a personal best score. Read the break and choose your line as you would any putt. Then—and this is important—commit to it. Set up to the ball along the line you've chosen. Force yourself not to second-guess the line you chose as you stood or squatted behind the ball. A key difference between amateurs and professionals is that a Tour pro rarely waffles in his decision making. Once the line has been chosen, a Tour pro will set up to that line, then forget about it. His focus instantly moves to the speed of the putt and the target. Far too many amateurs, once they assume their address, shuffle their feet or manipulate their putterhead because they lose trust in the line they've selected. That loss of trust will hurt you every time. Putt at least 10 practice balls with the intent to build trust in your green reading. Choose a line, set up to that line, and make your stroke.

It's crucial that, during your trusting practice, you go through your preputt routine in its entirety. A consistent stroke starts with a consistent preshot routine. Often, the Tour players with whom I work will go through their preputt motions and, just prior to making their strokes, back off and start their routines over again. They do this if they feel they've lost their commitment to the line or their focus. The goal is to maintain focus and a commitment to the line, and to address every putt the same way every time without fail. By doing so, they grow comfortable with the act of putting. It becomes as natural as walking, which ultimately causes them to relax and truly focus on the task at hand.

Practice for Touch

Great putters talk a lot about the importance of having "soft hands." Soft hands means having light grip pressure, which allows you to feel your putterhead and get reliable feedback about the "solidness" of contact from your putter. Great putters consistently roll the ball at the ideal speed. Many good putters, like Jack Nicklaus, believe successful putting depends on having good feel for distance and has little to do with mechanics. A few players think feel and touch can't be learned, or can improve only so much with practice. Most players believe that feel and touch can be mastered through learning how to relax and ridding the hands of tension. Remember, the key to less tension in the hands is less tension in the forearms.

No matter how much feel or touch is in you, most great putters rely on specific drills to improve their touch. The level of touch and feel you develop ultimately depends on how much you practice to improve touch.

Trusting Your Stroke

There's a school of thought that says you shouldn't practice short putts before you play. The theory behind this type of thinking is that if you miss a few short practice putts, you'll build fear and lower your confidence when faced with similar putts out on the course. I disagree with this line of thought for one simple reason: if you're unable to trust yourself before a round, you'll have a difficult time trusting yourself as you play. I would prefer that you practice a few short putts before you tee off so that you'll be more comfortable on the course.

It's okay if you happen to miss a couple during your preround confidence practice. The key is to not focus on negative outcomes. Forget missed putts. Become comfortable with the fact that you're not going to make every putt you look at. Do, however, congratulate yourself for putts made. Store the image of the ball rolling in the hole in your memory bank as you warm up. Then, when you're on the course, pull up the image of success as you walk through your preputt routine. Missing nine out of 10 practice putts should leave you, at the very least, with one mental image of a successful stroke. Usually that's enough to build the trust necessary for the course.

So hit a few short putts, three at a time. Then move on to six- to eight-footers, again, three balls at a time. Last, putt a few breaking 20-footers, this time with only one ball. Here's where you should focus on the speed of the green and how a putt reacts to the slope and grain. Remember to putt each ball as you would on the course. Use your preputt routine every time. Store successes in your mind.

While you're practicing these three-, six-, and 20-footers, it's not a bad idea to focus on your breathing. If you're typical of most weekend players, you'll approach a breaking five-footer to save par with more fear than you would a 200-yard approach over water. Correct breathing will help calm your nerves and, as a result, your stroke. As you stand over each putt, take a deep breath. Slowly exhale just prior to beginning

TOM WATSON—A LIGHTS-OUT PUTTER

With eight major championships (including five British Opens), five PGA Tour money titles, and three Vardon Trophies (for low scoring average) to his credit, Tom Watson is clearly one of the greatest of all time. However, after winning 32 events between 1974 and 1987, Watson went nine years without a victory, until his emotional win at the 1996 Memorial Tournament. The simple reason for this protracted slump was putting.

During his heyday, Watson was an extremely aggressive putter, making bold runs at long putts with the confidence that he could hole any comebacker. He believed that the majority of bad putts resulted from deceleration at impact and he concentrated on being aggressive with his stroke through the ball. Watson accomplished this by taking a short backstroke and giving the ball an authoritative strike with a longer forward stroke. The technique worked, especially during his historic hot streak between '77 and '81 when he won 23 PGA events.

Unfortunately, during his slump, Watson lost the ability to be aggressive through the ball.

Without this ability, his confidence faded, particularly on short putts, which naturally led to a more tentative stroke on longer attempts.

For much of his career, Watson favored the Ping Pal putter. Later, he switched to an Odyssey heel-toe model with a softer face and reclaimed some of his former magic, winning the Memorial in '96 and the Colonial in '98. In only his second Senior Tour event, Watson bagged the '99 Bank One Championship, needing only 79 putts to complete all three rounds.

your stroke. Feel your arms and hands relax as you set your putterhead into motion.

Trusting Yourself

PGA Tour player Scott McCarron ends his confidence or preround practice sessions by stroking a few putts with his eyes closed. After reading the putt and taking his stance, he'll close his eyes, holding the image of the target in his mind's eye. Putting with your eyes closed is the ultimate trust-builder. It's also a great way to better your target retention and learn to putt with feel rather than fear. Plus, with your eyes closed, you'll be able to better resist the temptation to rotate your head as you make contact with the ball to see where your putt is headed. Moving your head will almost guarantee that you'll move your putterhead off-line. Sam Snead never looked up until—hopefully—he heard the ball drop into the hole. Give the Slammer's technique a try. Close your eyes, breathe in, breathe out, and make your stroke. The familiar sound of the ball rattling in the bottom of the cup is the only indication of success you'll need.

6

Reading the Green

The art of appraising slope and speed—that is, of reading a green—can be derived only from experience.
—Bobby Jones

As we've seen throughout this book, there are a lot of pieces that make up lights-out putting. You need the right mental attitude, the right setup, solid stroke fundamentals, and a commitment to practice. Now add to that list the ability to read greens. Green reading—the art of finding the line and speed—is paramount for better performance. If the line and speed of a putt aren't considered, then a golfer is merely hoping to get the ball close to the hole. They're not planning to get the ball close to the hole. For most amateurs, gauging the slope and speed of their putts, except for the very short ones, remains a mystery. That's because green reading takes practice—there are nuances to the task that can only be mastered through trial, error, and familiarity. But I believe anyone can become a proficient green reader as long as he invests a little time and effort and knows what to look for.

Determining the line and speed of your putts should start well before you reach the green. In fact, from 20 to 30 yards away from the green is where you'll get the best perspective of how the green is set, the amount of tilt the green has, and the overall slope of the putting surface. All this information will give you valuable clues about the putt you're about to attempt and, more important, the line on which you want your ball to roll along: the line of putt.

Line of Putt Defined

The line of putt is an invisible or imagined line from your ball to the target—the line along which the ball must travel to reach and fall into the hole. According to the USGA's *Rules of Golf,* "This is the line that the player wishes his ball to take after a stroke on the putting green. It includes a reasonable distance on either side of the intended line but the line doesn't extend beyond the hole." The position of the ball on the green is the beginning of the line; the hole is the end of the line.

In reality, of course, this invisible line is not a line—it's more like a channel with boundaries within which the ball must travel. Look at the definition again. It says that it includes a reasonable distance on either side of the intended line.

With the hole being 4.25 inches in diameter and a regulation ball having a diameter of 1.68 inches, the ball doesn't have to follow a fine line to reach the hole, nor does it have to hit the dead center of the hole to go in. Normally, if just half the ball hits the hole, it will fall in. This adds another 0.84 inches of "drop" area to each side of the hole, making the hole appear to be about 3½ times as wide as the ball.

All of a sudden, the hole is a much larger target. With this seemingly larger hole at the end of the line of putt, the ball can waver a little off-line (staying within the channel) and still have a chance of dropping into the hole should at least half of the ball touch the cup's edge.

The line of putt is determined through careful analysis of many factors, the most important being speed and slope. The other factors play a lesser role, but still should be understood and applied when calculating this line.

Factors That Affect the Line

Putting is a combination of distance and direction. Which is more important? For most putts, distance control is more important than directional accuracy. If you reflect back on your recent misses, I'll bet the majority of them failed to drop because you didn't hit the putt the correct distance. Most golfers can find the correct break. The problem is that they can't control the speed of the putt to fit the line they chose. I see this mistake all the time. For example, on a 25-foot putt, most amateurs will be short or long of the hole by twice the margin of their aim.

This is unfortunate, since if you can't get the ball to the hole, or send it too far past the hole, you're not going to make very many putts. Additionally, if you stroke a putt with the wrong speed, you'll likely add to or subtract from the amount of break you read when you chose the line, increasing the likelihood of a nasty second putt and, often, a three-putt.

Getting the Speed Right

Determining the correct amount of speed involves knowing how long the putt is, the general pace of the green, and becoming familiar with

Planning Your Approaches

The best putters think about their putting strategy as they plan their approach shots. Where a player lands his shot makes a crucial difference in the number of strokes taken on or around the green. The size, shape, and even the texture of the green should determine where you want your ball to land. This explains why even the best players in the world won't always fire straight at the pin. Usually, they'll target their approach shots to areas that leave them with the easiest possible putt.

The best example of the importance of setting up the putt from the fairway is Augusta National. Seasoned players know that during the Masters, it's often better to have the right putt from 20 feet than the wrong putt from six feet. I've walked Augusta during several practice rounds, and I've always found it easy to pick out the veterans from the new kids. The golfers who do well on Augusta's nearly impossible greens take the time to study the putting surfaces well before the tournament begins. They practice their putting on areas of the green where they hope to hit their approach shots come tournament time. They look for areas that are "dead"—that is, positions that set up a difficult putt in relation to possible pin positions. Often, the winner of the Green Jacket is not the player who makes the most putts, but who three-putts the least. These players are those that target their approach shots based on the putt the shot will leave them.

the surrounding conditions. Determining the length of a putt is as easy as walking off the distance from the cup to your ball. I recommend that you do this for any putt over 10 feet. Only by knowing how long the putt is will you know how hard or softly to stroke the ball.

The Stimpmeter

Some greens are faster than others. But how much faster? Thanks to the Stimpmeter, pros—and amateurs—now have objective criteria to compare and contrast different putting surfaces.

The Stimpmeter was invented by Edward Stimpson, the 1935 Massachusetts Amateur champion. It's a simple device, consisting of a three-foot-long metal ramp with a chute down the middle and a notch at one end. To measure the speed of a green, a ball is loaded into the notch and the Stimpmeter is lifted until gravity forces the ball to roll down the chute and onto the putting surface. The procedure is then repeated in the opposite direction. The average length the ball rolls is the Stimpmeter reading.

At most Major championships, the Stimpmeter reading will be in the 10½–11-feet range, as it was at Pinehurst for the 1999 U.S. Open. However, at some venues, like Augusta National, the Stimpmeter reading can be as high as 13½ feet. If you've ever watched the Masters on TV, you've seen how fast Augusta's greens can be. Often, pros need only to tap their putts to get them rolling toward the hole on even a flat putt. You can imagine the difficulty when the putt is downhill or slides to the right or left.

Opponents of the Stimpmeter claim that its readings don't relate much to the recreational golfer. What's the difference between a green that's stimped at 10 versus a green that's stimped at 12? Most golfers lack the green-reading finesse to adjust to such detailed classifications. The best advice is to forget Stimpmeter readings and gauge the speed of the greens yourself on the practice putting green before your round. Plus, all Stimp readings are taken on flat portions of the putting green. And when was the last time you had an absolutely flat putt?

As we saw in Chapter 3, great putters adjust for putt length — and therefore speed — by adjusting the length of their backstrokes. Longer putts, which require greater ball speed, need longer backstrokes. The opposite holds true for shorter putts. The problem lies in matching backstroke length with putt length and speed. Unfortunately, I can't supply you with a backstroke length/speed conversion chart. Knowing how hard to hit your putts in order to roll the ball at a specific speed and a specific distance takes practice and familiarity with the greens you're playing on.

For an example of a way to dial in the correct stroke length to fit the speed and length of a given putt, watch Tiger Woods. As he sets up the ball, he takes a number of practice strokes. At this point, Tiger's not working on his stroke fundamentals. He's visualizing the ball rolling into the hole and experimenting with different stroke lengths, until, in his mind's eye, he finds the one he believes will roll the ball at the right speed and the right distance.

In addition to the overall length of a putt, green conditions determine a lot about how hard or soft you need to stroke your putts in order to get them close to the hole. As a rule, I follow the four primary "speed meters" to help me factor the speed at which I stroke all my putts. As you'll soon discover, there are other factors that affect speed, but these are the most dominant:

- Firm greens are faster than soft greens.
- Uphill putts are slower than downhill putts.
- Bent greens are faster than Bermuda greens.
- Putts toward the nearest body of water (or the nearest dominant geologic feature) are faster than putts in the opposite direction.

Note: Different ball speeds can affect the line of putt. Except for straight putts, there will never be a single correct line of putt, because different ball speeds require different lines of putt on the same slope. Depending on how hard you like to hit the ball, you may have to lower the amount of break you read into a putt for a faster ball, or raise it for a slower one. Most of the time, I advise students to play the high road (play more break), as it will allow them to stroke the putt more slowly and leave the ball closer to the hole for an easy two-putt.

On a sloping putt, take the high road. Play for more break than you expect, and strike the putt a little softer, especially when the green is fast. You'll leave yourself with an easier second putt should you miss than if you played less break and struck the putt with more force.

Determining Slope

Like the speed, if slope isn't considered, putting becomes a matter of luck. According to Webster's Tenth New Collegiate Dictionary, slope is defined as an "upward or downward slant or inclination." In golfing terms, it means the slant of the green. Slope is important because it's the critical factor that determines if your line of putt travels right-to-left or left-to-right, or is straight.

If you hit a ball toward a hole without considering slope, you'll get close only if there's little break and if you've hit it hard enough to overcome the slope. If the ball isn't hit hard enough or doesn't go in the right direction, it will fall short or break away from the hole and may end up farther away than where you started.

Like most aspects of putting, the only real way to determine slope is through practice. All I can do is provide you with clues as to how your ball will react in different situations. When calculating the slope of any

GREG NORMAN—A LIGHTS-OUT PUTTER

Possibly the greatest putt in Greg Norman's storied career came in the 1984 U.S. Open at Winged Foot. It was the 72nd hole of the tournament, and The Shark needed to sink a 45-foot, downhill twister for birdie to get into a play-off with Fuzzy Zoeller. Norman made that incredibly difficult putt by aiming his putterface not at the cup, but at a discolored spot on the green along his line of putt.

This technique—picking out a point at the very apex of the break and using that as the target instead of the hole—is called apex (or spot) putting. Norman uses this technique because he feels that once the ball gets past the apex, or highest point of the break, he can no longer control it. So instead of concerning himself with the hole, he concentrates on getting the ball to the apex with the proper speed to take it to the hole.

Obviously, apex putting has paid Norman great dividends. Not only is he the PGA Tour's leading money winner all-time (with over $11 million dollars in earnings through 1999), but he's also one of its greatest champions, with two British Open titles and more than 70 professional victories.

Over the years, The Shark has favored a stainless-steel Ping Anser 2 and the classic Wilson 8802, which he used in his 1986 British Open victory and his scorching 267 at Royal St. George's in 1993. In 1986, Norman's trusty 8802 helped him card birdie or eagle on an amazing one out of every four holes.

green, use the following rules. By understanding these guidelines, you'll get a better idea of how to plan for left-to-right break, right-to-left break, or no break at all.

- Uphill putts add to the effective distance of the putt compared with a level putt, because of gravity pushing against the ball.
- Downhill putts reduce the effective distance, because gravity slings it farther than if the ground were level.
- The greater the slope, the more the ball's roll will be affected.
- The faster the ball speed, the less the effect of the slope.
- A slope near the origination of the putt will have less effect than when the slope is near the hole.
- The shorter the cut of grass (a faster green), the more the slope will affect the putt, because there's less friction against the ball.
- Sidehill putts tend to sling the ball farther left or right than golfers expect, often because the ball speed is slower than normal.

Other Factors That Affect the Line

In addition to the speed and the slope, there are several other variables to consider when determining the line of putt. An inherent knowledge of these fringe effects can transform a good putter into a lights-out putter when it comes to reading the green. Experience is always the best teacher, but here are a few general rules to follow under certain conditions:

Multiple Slopes

Reading a putt that crosses over several slopes is difficult even for the professional. For most golfers, it's best to consider just the slope near the hole, since that slope will have more of an effect than the slope nearest the ball. The reason I say this is that as the ball slows it will be more influenced by the slope, and the ball will be moving more slowly as it approaches the cup than it does as it leaves the putterface.

Grain

Grain is nothing more than the prevailing direction in which the grass blades are growing. This can cause friction against the ball when putting into the grain. The ball sort of floats over the grain when putting with the grain's flow. The green's grain can affect the roll of the ball almost as much as a mild slope, and it can turn a mild slope into a severe slope if the grain grows in the direction of the slope. Conversely, the grain can diminish the effects of the slope if it runs counter to the slope.

Rules of Grain

- The longer the cut of grass, the greater the effect of grain; play less break if the slope goes against the grain.
- The shorter the cut of grass, the less the effect of grain.
- Putting into the grain can add to the overall distance of the putt; a 15-foot putt may play like an 18-foot putt.
- Putting with the grain can decrease the overall distance of the putt; a 20-foot putt may play like a 15-footer.
- Bermuda grass greens have more grain than bent-grass greens; find out what you're playing on.

The direction in which grass grows (grain), as well as its thickness and height, will have varying effects on a putt. To become a better putter, you must understand how grain affects your ball. Putts will roll faster and farther, gliding easily across the top of the grass, when the grass blades are turned away from the ball. This is called "with the grain" or "downgrain." Putts roll more slowly when the grass blades are turned toward the ball. The ball butts up against the grass, causing it to quickly slow down. This is called "against the grain" or "upgrain." Putts that must roll diagonally across the grass blades will normally break in the direction the grass is growing. This is called "cross-grain."

Where grain is concerned, experience, again, is definitely the best teacher. If the greens mower has been hard at work, it's very difficult to determine the direction of grain. One neat trick is to stand somewhere behind your ball while looking at the hole, and notice whether the green surface has a shiny or dull appearance.

With the Grain: If you see a shine (surface appears light or silvery), it means that the grass is growing away from you and you'll be putting with the grain. In this case, your ball will travel farther with less effort on your part.

Against the Grain: If you see little or no shine (surface appears dark, dirty, or dull), it means you'll be putting against the grain and you must use an extra-firm stroke to make your ball reach the hole.

Cross-Grain: If the surface in front of you appears to have a combination of shine and no shine, it probably means that you'll be putting across the grain. It's difficult enough to understand any grain definition, let alone cross-grain, so if you have trouble with the concept of grain, don't worry about it until you've made significant improvement in your putting game. Just treat cross-grain putts like straight ones for the time being.

Sometimes the weather or even the time of day can make it difficult to decide whether there's a shine on the green's surface. So if it's cloudy or late in the day, look at the way the grass grows around the hole and you may find a clue as to grain direction. Grass will lie across the edge of the hole in the direction it's growing. If the grass is overhanging the front edge of the hole (and away from you), you'll be putting with the grain. Conversely, if the grass is growing away from the front edge (and toward you), you'll be putting against the grain. Also, become aware of mower grain. Grass mowers can alter a green's inherent grain. Typically, a mower influences grain in the direction it moves on each pass across the green.

Another trick to understanding the differences in shine is to find a thick carpet and try some experiments. If you brush down the carpet nap, the carpet will appear bright and shiny (with the grain). If you brush against the nap, the carpet will appear dark and less shiny (against the grain). If you brush across the nap, one side will appear shinier than the other (cross-grain). With practice you'll learn how to translate these experiments into reading grain on the course. However, please remember that the *Rules of Golf* don't allow you to brush the grass during a competitive round. That's testing the surface, and will cost you two strokes or a loss of hole.

Grass Height

If the grass has just been mowed, the ball will roll faster than when the grass blades are long. An uncut green played early in the morning can be very slow and can require a much harder stroke than in the afternoon, when the sun has dried things off.

Damp or Wet Grass

A damp or wet green can cause your putt to break less than the apparent slope indicates. Whether there's a light or heavy covering of water, the greens will be slower and the ball won't roll as far, or break as much, as on dry greens when you use a normal stroke. You have to stroke the ball more firmly than normal. With time and practice, you'll learn the best way to play under wet conditions.

Dave Pelz, author of Putt Like the Pros, gives a tip for playing in the rain: "When you mark your ball, remove it from the surface and dry it carefully. Then replace it gently so only the small part of the ball touching the green gets wet. Concentrate on stroking the ball as squarely as possible on the line you intend, with no sidespin. If you can do this, as the ball rolls along, only the center will get wet. This makes the ball heavier around the center, and it will roll straight and truer (a gyroscopic effect). Remember to play for less break, keep your stroke firm, and use wetness to your advantage."

Grass Types

If you're a studious golfer and want to know as much as possible about green conditions, knowledge of grass types used on the greens can be helpful in finding grain and establishing your line of putt. But for most golfers, knowing the type of grass won't mean much. I've noted below the basic characteristics of two very common grass types used on golf courses—namely, Bermuda and bent grass.

Bermuda grass is used extensively in the South, Southwest, Caribbean area, and Southern California because it grows well in hot climates. The grass is very grainy, wiry, bristly, and stubby to the touch. This makes for a coarse putting surface. It's difficult to see the grain of Bermuda grass when simply looking at the blades; if you remember nothing else, remember the key characteristic of Bermuda grass is that it grows toward the setting sun, east to west.

Bent grass is widely used in the United States along both seacoasts and in the North, Northeast, and Midwest. It grows toward mountains and away from water. Bent grass is naturally short-bladed and has very little grain. Generally, bent grasses provide a slick, smooth putting surface when closely mowed. If you're playing on bent grasses that are difficult to read, it's safe to assume that the grass grows toward the lowest side of the green where the water drains.

Mother Nature

All other effects considered, the environment surrounding the courses on which you play can determine the direction your ball travels once it's struck. Since courses differ from one area to the next, it's always a good idea to ask the local pro if any environmental factors come into play on that particular course. This local knowledge is invaluable. If time is limited or the pro is unavailable, make use of the following rules of thumb. They outline the possible effects Mother Nature can have on your putts.

- Putts tend to break (or move faster) toward surrounding mountains.
- Putts tend to break (or move faster) toward the nearest water, whether it's a lake, pond, river, or the Pacific Ocean.
- Putts tend to break (or move faster) toward obvious drainage areas; look for particularly wet sections around the green or flood channels.
- Putts tend to break (or move faster) toward the sun, because grass grows toward the sunshine, enhancing the effect of grain.

Ground Control

After analyzing the green for speed, slope grain, and other external factors, carefully inspect the proposed line of putt and pick up any impediments that could affect the roll of the ball. Be careful not to touch the line of putt—penalty strokes can be incurred by doing so.

According to the USGA's *Rules of Golf*, the line of putt must not be touched, except that you may:

- move sand and loose soil on the green and other loose impediments (defined as natural objects such as stones, leaves, twigs, branches, and the like; dung, worms, insects and casts or heaps made by them, provided they are not fixed or growing, are not solidly embedded, and do not adhere to the ball) by picking them up or by brushing them aside with your hand or a club, without pressing anything down (casual water cannot be brushed aside). Dew and frost are not loose impediments.

- place the putterhead in front of the ball without pressing anything down
- press down a ball marker
- lift the ball when marking or cleaning it
- measure the distance between the ball and the hole
- repair old hole plugs or ball marks (spike marks, cup imperfections, and other damage to the green's surface cannot be repaired until everyone has completed the hole)
- remove movable obstructions

Finding Your Final Line of Putt

When calculating the final line, you must first survey the green before you reach it—you'll always see the slope of the green better walking up to it rather than when you're on it (devout cart riders take note). Hopefully, you've already developed a feel for the speed of the greens on the practice putting green. To best calculate the slope, always begin your read from behind the ball. From this position, look to see if the ground between you and the hole slants to the left, to the right, or is flat. To confirm your initial read, walk to the low side of the hole (if there is one). This will also give you a quick visual as to whether the ground between your ball and the hole is uphill, downhill, or flat.

If you don't feel confident about your read at this point, take a look at the putt from behind the hole, although your reads from behind the ball and from the low side of the hole will usually provide you with all the information you need. Don't overanalyze your read. Not only does this slow down the pace of play, but it may add to your indecision and fuel a loss of commitment. In my opinion, your first, or instinctual, read will be your best.

Once you've determined which direction the putt will break, you must calculate how much it will break. This is where speed and slope come together to produce the break point (or apex point). This is the point where the ball will "break" and start rolling toward the hole.

With the break point identified, you'll be able to determine a fairly accurate line of putt, one that starts from the position of your ball, rises up to the break point (if there is one), and curves down to the hole. Given the proper ball speed, you'll be able to roll the ball along your

To get the most accurate read of the slope, sight your putt from behind the ball and from the low side of the hole.

line of putt, over the break point—wherever it may be—and down into the hole.

A mistake I see many amateurs make is asking their partners or caddies to determine the breaks of their putts. The problem here is that if you rely on other people to read putts for you, you'll never learn and experience the skills required for gauging break and speed, and you'll limit the amount of trust you can place in your abilities. I know that Tour players rely on caddies when it comes time to reading the green. But the situation on the Tour is a lot different from your experiences as a golfer. For one, it's a caddy's job to know the greens. Second, a Tour caddy knows his player's tendencies inside and out. Together, they are a team, a unit that gets better and better at green reading the longer they work together. I doubt that your playing partners or caddy, if and when you have the opportunity to use one, has this type of familiarity with your putting game. If you ask your partner to read the break, they'll give it to you based on the speed they hit their putts, not yours. The bottom line is that you need to read your own putts. Ask for advice only when you're truly confused.

Finding the Break Point

Finding the break point is the critical element in aligning your putt. Again, this is the maximum height the ball must rise before turning toward the hole along the line of putt. In determining the break point, remember: break is in the eye of the beholder. Your eyes are the key to finding the break point. Unfortunately, only by experience will you be able to find the exact break point for a sloping putt. The best advice is to keep things simple. If you calculate the slope as left-to-right, then target your break point to the left of the hole. Knowing how far out to position the break point will come in time. If you familiarize yourself with the rules of speed, slope, grain, and the other external factors that affect the line of putt, your ability to accurately position the break point will blossom.

This fact understates the importance of "watching" the ball. When you or your partners hit your chips and pitches, watch how the ball reacts once it lands. This can tell you a lot about the speed and degree of slope you'll face when you set up for the putt. Once on the green, make sure you watch the putts of the other players in your group. The more you can become familiar with how the ball reacts on different putting surfaces, the more accurate you'll be in determining the break point for your putt.

One method to finding the break point, is "seeing the line." Crouch behind the ball, select a break point then, in your mind's eye, set the ball in motion. Watch the ball reach the break point—revolution by revolution—then bend back toward the cup. This sounds rather simple, but don't underestimate the power of imagination. You've likely seen hundreds of putts before. You have a general idea of how they react to certain degrees of slope. So does your mind. You'll find that when you practice "seeing the line," your mind will instinctively tell you if you played enough break.

What About Plumb Bobbing?

For some, plumb bobbing is a very accurate system of determining the slant of the green. When you plumb-bob correctly, you'll actually be able to see the slant of the green and you'll be able to visualize the break point. The first step to learning the art of plumb bobbing is to discover which eye is the dominant one. If you use the wrong eye, plumb bobbing will never work.

To find your dominant eye, extend both arms straight out in front of your face and form a triangle between your thumbs and index fingers. Aim the triangle at an object about 15 feet away. Now close only your left eye. If the landmark appears to jump out of the triangle when you close your left eye, then you're left-eye dominant. If your object remains fixed when you close your left eye, then you're right-eye dominant.

To perform the plumb-bob technique, stand approximately four to five feet behind your ball and find the baseline—the line extending from the hole back to the ball. (On shorter putts, reduce the distance to two or three feet.) Facing the hole, straddle this line. Position your feet at shoulder-width apart. Be sure your stance is centered directly over the baseline. Now squat down. You can plumb-bob while standing, but in my experience, it provides the best read from a squatting position. If your knees can handle squatting, you'll gain a better perspective of the slope.

Grasp the putter handle near the bottom of the grip or where it's comfortable. Hold the putter at arm's length between your thumb and forefinger, and raise or lower the putter so that the center of the grip is level with your eyes. Maintain a light grip and let the shaft hang freely. Don't tighten your grip. The toe of the

To find your dominant eye, make a triangle with your thumbs and forefingers and capture an object in the distance. If you close your left eye and the object jumps out of the triangle, then you're left eye dominant.

What About Plumb Bobbing? (continued)

putter should face the hole. Hold the putter so that the lower part of the shaft bisects the ball. Now close your non-dominant eye. Run your open dominant eye up the shaft and sight the putt. Note the relationship of the puttershaft to the hole. This is the maximum height the ball must rise before turning toward the hole. This is the break point.

Unless the putt is straight, the hole will become visible either to the left or right of the putter shaft. If the hole appears to be to the left of the shaft, the ground slopes right-to-left. If the hole appears to be to the right of the shaft, the ground slopes left-to-right. If the shaft covers the hole, there's no break and you've got a straight putt.

When you plumb-bob, you'll get the most accurate read of whether the green slopes left-to-right, right-to-left (as shown), or is flat.

Although plumb bobbing will give you a good idea of where the break point lies, understand that the exact location of the break point is dependent on the speed, grain, and texture of the grass.

During my short-game schools, I like to play a little game with the students in an effort to teach them to read greens. I'll choose a 20-foot breaking putt and will ask each student in the group to read the break. After I've placed tees where each student feels the break point of the putt lies, I'll place my tee where I believe it is. My tee has never indicated less than a third more break than what the students read, often more than twice as much.

Of course, I'll demonstrate and hit the putt with less speed, playing more break. The end result is that when the ball stops rolling, if it isn't in the cup, it's right around the cup for an easy two-putt.

The baseline is a line that runs from your ball to the hole. The line of putt is the line on which your ball will actually travel to the hole, given the effects of slope. When the baseline and the line of putt are the same, you've got a straight putt.

When the average player reads breaks, his or her attention is usually focused on the hole rather than the speed and the actual breaking point of the putt. The danger of playing less break with more speed is that when the ball stops rolling, the player is left with one of those three- to four-foot knee-knocking putts—unless, of course, they get lucky and the ball slams into the back of the cup.

When students are closer than four feet to the hole, I encourage them to play the putt with less break and more speed, within reason. Again, when I see a player three-putt, it's usually the result of not hitting the putt with the correct speed. My standard answer to players who feel they miss too many three- to four-footers is that they have too many three- to four-footers in the first place. With the proper speed, any golfer can putt the ball close enough for an easy tap-in.

The most important thing to remember is that once you're past eight to 10 feet, speed becomes the most important factor in reading the break of your putts.

Determining the Final Line

The final line of putt refers to the imaginary line, or channel, calculated using the techniques covered in this chapter. I selected speed and slope as being the most important variables in this calculation. In many cases, depending on your putting abilities, you may look for grain or grass type first. You have to be the judge as to which variables you'll consider for your putts. I recommend that speed determination be your first and foremost concern. When your putting style improves, you can refine your calculations and add the effects of the other variables.

If you don't find any break, don't always assume the putt will be straight. In my opinion, there are very few straight putts in golf, especially those that are more than four feet long.

Once your calculations are complete, and you've found the break point (if there is one), pick an intermediate target that's on a line from your ball to the break point. Often, the break point will be more than several feet away, making the task of aiming the putterface at it difficult. Pick a spot no more than six inches in front of your ball and align to it. You'll find that it's much easier to align to a spot six inches away than one that's six feet away.

Bowlers use the same type of alignment strategy. If you've ever bowled, you know about the spots that are a few feet in front of you on the lane. You look at the spots and then pick a line to roll the ball over. Strike!

Another strategy to help you better align your putts is to take the logo on your golf ball and set it along the line that you want the putt to follow. This can help you get a better visual reference of the line. Many players on the Tour, like Brad Faxon and Tiger Woods, take a Sharpie pen and make a line about one inch in length along the equator of the ball. You can use this method the same way you use the logo on your ball. Both techniques can help you achieve a better visual reference for stroking the ball down the intended path. When you stand over the putt, the ball is already aimed.

Final Thoughts

The line of putt is only final in the sense that you intend to make the putt. If you take several strokes to get into the hole, then each time your ball position changes, you need to establish a new line. This applies to putts of all lengths. Too many golfers will carefully line up long putts and then fail to use the same procedure on short ones. I suppose they conclude that the short line of putt is straight and that a hard stroke will send the ball into the center of the hole. Since truly straight putts are rare, experience shows that even the short putt requires the same concentration as the long putt, if not more.

Above all, stay committed! Once you've selected your final line of putt and have established the direction and speed necessary to get close to or into the hole, don't change your mind. If you have any doubt at the last minute just before you take your backstroke, stop everything. Step back. Reevaluate what you're about to do. Look at the putt as if from a new ball position. I realize this is difficult and you may think it's a waste of time, but you must proceed slowly and carefully. It will pay off. This strategy should come into play throughout your game.

A Few Keys

At the start of this chapter, I mentioned that properly reading the green is an art form. As such, it takes practice. We've covered a lot of information over the last few pages, so I don't expect you to green-read right away like a Phi Beta Kappa. As a start, work on the following green-reading fundamentals. Once you have these down pat, simply let experience become your guide.

- Take a good look at the whole green as you approach it. Often I find that from a distance I can get a pretty good idea of the lie of the land, and that's my first clue as to what breaks the ball might take.
- Look from behind the ball and look from the side. It needn't take a long time—if you're smart, you can usually find time in between your playing partners' approach shots and putts.
- Look at what your playing partner's ball does as it approaches the hole. Even if he isn't coming from exactly the same line as you, you can still learn a lot about how the ball behaves in that crucial last 18 inches or so of its journey to the hole.
- Remember, speed determines break. A firmly struck putt breaks less than a ball hit at a slower speed. So decide how firmly you want to hit the putt, then establish how much the ball will move at that speed. In the end, you should leave yourself with a tap-in should you miss the cup.
- Some golfers find it hard to believe that wind can affect the line of a putt, but it does. Obviously, a light breeze isn't going to do anything, but if your trouser bottoms are flapping, then that should alert you to the fact that it's strong enough to make a difference. And the faster the greens, the more the wind will influence the ball's path to the hole. It can cancel out the break on some putts, or increase the swing on others.

Finally, experiment a little. I can't show you the break on putts, so the best thing you can do is work on a trial-and-error basis. During your next practice session, drop some balls around a hole—say, three to six feet—and try to read each putt individually. Then hit the putt and see if you were right. If you read it incorrectly, take a second look and see if you can see the line now. Bit by bit, you're training your eyes to spot the telltale signs. And that really is what reading greens is all about. You can't just suddenly become a good line-reader overnight. Like anything else, it takes practice and experience.

7

Strategy, Tactics, Rules, and Etiquette

"I have a tip that can take five strokes off anyone's golf game. It's called an eraser."
—**Arnold Palmer**

The ability to score well develops with practice. Like I've stated throughout this book, improvements in your game can't happen overnight. Nor can improvements in your score. Nevertheless, with the tips provided thus far, you're well on your way to posting your best scores very soon. You won't require an eraser to drop strokes. Your putting will take care of that on its own.

The mental, physical, and emotional skills of lights-out putting, when fully developed, set the stage for improved performance. The putter will ultimately become your most deadly weapon, an instrument to strike fear in the hearts of your opponents. But there's more you can accomplish on the course with your trusty blade or mallet than simply holing putts. Your putter and putting stroke can help you out of a myriad of difficult situations on the course. So, too, can your knowledge of the rules of the green and the strategic implementation of your putter in different situations. In this chapter, we'll put the finishing touches on your putting game. Specifically, we'll break down the tactics, rules, and etiquette procedures that will transform you from a lights-out putter to a lights-out putting machine.

Great players differentiate themselves from great ballstrikers with their ability to work the ball and to create opportunities using their imagination. Great putters differentiate themselves from players who putt great by creating opportunities with their putters and putting strokes in situations where they typically aren't considered an option.

By familiarizing yourself with and practicing these techniques, you'll round out your qualifications as a lights-out putter and send your game soaring to unforeseen heights.

The following are time-honored skills great putters use to score their best. Many are techniques, whereas others represent a more in-depth knowledge of the game itself. Regardless, each has the potential ability to save you costly strokes during each and every round.

Strategic Shots

During the course of your golfing career, you're going to face a lot of different kinds of putts. You'll come across nasty little five-footers, multiple slopes, straight-as-the-crow-flies uphillers, and speedy, sliding downhill putts, to name a few. Many players view any putt other than "straight up and straight in" as a true test, a state of mind that encourages their fear and increases the tension in their stroke. In my opinion, there's no reason why you need to shiver in your spikes when faced with a tough putt.

The same goes for your shots around the green. A lights-out putter should be in command of the green and its environs. This includes bunkers, the apron, the fringe, whatever. Your putting game, in a sense, will ultimately feed off the success of your short game, which is why I advise players to practice their putting first, then immediately go to the practice chipping green.

In addition to your stroke fundamentals and your practice of the standard collection of putts, chips, pitches, and bunker blasts, I'd like you to perfect the strategic shots listed below. They'll help you in the areas of putting in which amateurs are typically the least skilled. They'll also aid your short game in situations where the usual techniques don't apply. Work these short-game supershots into your practice routine. That way, you'll be prepared to face anything the course gives you during the match. And that's a type of confidence great players strive to develop.

Lag Putting

Of all the different types of putts there are in the world of golf, none gives amateurs more fits than the lengthy lag putt. Forty feet, 50 feet, 60 feet: putts from these lengths result in more three-putts than two-putts for most players.

Lagging a long putt into one-putt range is a special skill. Conventional wisdom advises golfers to aim their approach putts into a three-foot circle around the cup. I ask my players to try to make all putts, regardless of length. Go for the cup. If you happen to miss, you'll probably miss within three to five feet anyway, unless your read of the line was completely out of whack. A secondary quest should be to leave the ball, if you do happen to miss, on the low side of the hole. But even this strategy shouldn't deter you from trying to make the putt.

The next time you're faced with a long putt, stop yourself from saying "I just hope to get this close enough to tap it in." If you tell yourself this, you'll create too large a target, causing your focus to get a little sloppy. From 30 to 50 feet, your obvious goal is a two-putt, but that will be more easily accomplished if you try for a one-putt. And who knows, you may just make it.

Hopefully, with the instruction in this book, you'll develop the "I can make everything" attitude. If so, then you won't have to concern yourself with second putts when you have to lag. If you possess confidence and believe that you'll make that second putt regardless of where your first putt positions you, you'll free up your body and mind to go for the long bomb.

Toeing Downhill Putts

It's amazing to watch what fast greens can do to even the world's best golfers. The next time the Masters Tournament rolls around, pay particular attention to what goes on around the putting green. The slick, smooth putting surfaces of Augusta National typically wear down player confidence, especially on downhill putts. That's because Masters competitors know that a downhill putt, if missed, can leave a second putt as long as the first.

In order to combat the dangers of a fast downhill putt, many players set up to strike the putt on the toe of the putter rather than on the sweet spot. Hitting the ball on the toe will help "deaden" the putt. A ball hit on the toe will roll far less than a putt hit in the center with the same stroke. So instead of making a tiny tap on the ball (which is difficult to execute with accuracy under intense pressure), players will toe their putts. The softer roll is typically easier to control and usually produces the best results.

The next time you practice your putting, roll a few toed putts. Get a feel for how the ball reacts, and how far it rolls compared to putts struck in the center of the putterface. Put this technique into your arsenal of shots. You'll find that it comes in handy not only on downhill putts, put on severe left-to-right and right-to-left sliders.

Toeing a putt can help deaden your ball's roll, making it easy to control distance on difficult downhill putts.

Putting From the Bunker

Gary Player is known as one of the best bunker players ever. His artistry in the sand is second to none. But even Player, who can hole out with a sand wedge from almost any lie, will opt for the putter from a trap if the conditions are right.

Say you're in a shallow greenside bunker, and there's little green between the edge of the bunker and the cup. Flying a sand wedge onto the green from this situation is difficult if you're looking to get it close. Inspect the sand. If it's firm, simply use your putter. Set up as you would a normal putt, but play the ball a bit forward in your stance, and make your everyday stroke. If you catch the putt correctly, you'll find that it will roll over the sand quite easily (this technique is even more useful if the sand is wet). Don't give the putt too much; the ball will travel as fast as it would on a slow, shaggy green.

Another play from the bunker involves the situation when your ball is buried near the lip. Some instructors advise using the toe of the putter to knock the ball out. Although I'm in favor of using the putter as a strategic weapon, I don't think recreational players should try to blast a ball out of a bunker with their putter. In my opinion, the chances of the ball further embedding itself in the turf are far greater than its landing safely on the green. In this situation, stick with your sand wedge and close down the face.

The Chip Putting Stroke

Golf swings. If you've spent any time at all at a golf course or practice range, you know they come in many different sizes, styles, and speeds, with some occurring at a greater frequency than others. A keen eye, however, will tell you that golf swings come in only two shapes: linear and circular. Full and pitch swings are circular motions; putts and chips are linear. Knowing the difference can save you a lot of strokes around the green.

Ironically, there's only one club in your bag that's specifically designed for linear swings: the putter. The putter is the most upright of all your clubs, with a lie angle ranging anywhere from 70 to 74 degrees (and up to 80 degrees for a long putter). Putters are designed with such high lie angles so that the golfer, as he or she stands over the putt, is closer to the ball. Such proximity makes it easier to swing the putter back and forth in a relatively straight line.

All the other clubs in your set are designed to make circular swings. As such, the lie angles of these clubs are much flatter than for a putter. (A typical lie angle for a 6-iron, for example, is only 61 degrees.) A flatter lie angle forces you to stand farther away from the ball and swing around your body to generate power.

You probably don't consider these design differences when swinging a golf club, because you should never need to putt with a 3-iron or take a full swing with your putter. However, it's often necessary to execute chip shots of varying lengths with every club in your bag, including your woods. In order to pull off these score-saving chips, which, as I mentioned earlier, are linear motions, you need to transform the club you're using into a linear club, making it more of a putter than an iron or wood. You can do this by simply by raising the heel of the club off the ground. This naturally makes the club more upright (with a greater lie angle) and allows you to stand closer to the ball.

Go grab any chipping club and a putter from your bag. Set your putter and your chipping club side by side. Now raise the heel of the chipping club until the two shafts parallel each other. The chipping club is now set up for a linear swing.

By definition, a chip shot should spend little time in the air. The majority of the length it travels should be while the ball is rolling on the ground. In order to achieve such a trajectory, you need to chip the ball with a descending blow. If you set up correctly, you'll swing the club you're chipping with in such a manner naturally.

The first setup key is ball position. Place the ball opposite your back foot. This will ensure that the ball, not the ground, is struck first. Since you've increased the lie of the club by raising the heel, stand closer to the ball, leaving only two to three clubheads between the ball and the tips of your feet. At first this will seem awkward—you'll feel crowded. Stick with it—the results will be worthwhile.

The next step is to position your nose, sternum, and hands in front of the ball. This move places the majority of your weight on your front foot. This is essential to produce a descending stroke. A helpful thought here is to keep your shoulders level. If your front shoulder is higher than your rear shoulder, your weight distribution will be too neutral. This can cause thin or fat shots. Assume your setup in front of a mirror to check if your shoulders are level. If your arms are comfortably bent at the elbows, and close to your body, this position will be easy to attain.

All that remains is to swing the club with a smooth pendulum motion of the arms and shoulders, just as you would with your putter. A chipping stroke is a gentle stroke. The amount of effort required will be nearly identical to that required for a putt of the same distance.

The arms are the key to this type of stroke, just as they are in the putting stroke. They should move in a back-and-forth fashion, keeping the clubhead low to the ground and propelling it through the ball. The shoulders should merely respond to the pendulous motion of the arms, and your wrists should remain passive. Note that passive does not mean stiff: stay relaxed, or you'll risk losing touch and distance control.

JACK NICKLAUS—A LIGHTS-OUT PUTTER

Most people list Jack Nicklaus as the greatest golfer of all time. His trademark power fade and sheer determination ushered in a new era of golf. His power set a new standard, an asset that helped him outdrive his competitors by as much as 30 yards. But the characteristic that allowed Nicklaus to be so good, and for so long, was his willingness to purposely experiment and change on the putting green.

Jack Nicklaus wasn't a mechanical putter. He'd do anything to sink a putt, changing his setup and stroke from tournament to tournament, and sometimes even from green to green or putt to putt. The reason for this was that Nicklaus believed touch was the key to great putting.

Accordingly, Nicklaus used square-to-square, open-to-closed, and closed-to-open putting strokes, depending on how he was feeling and what was working that day. Because of his tendency to change styles, Nicklaus used a variety of

Jack Nicklaus—A Lights-Out Putter (continued)

putters, often bringing several to a tournament site and choosing his weapon the night before. However, the two putters most closely associated with the Golden Bear are the George Low Wizard 600, a flanged-blade model that he used for much of the early part of his career, and the oversized, heel-toe-weighted MacGregor ZT-615 with which he won the '86 Masters. During that particular tournament, Nicklaus dazzled the crowd and the millions watching on TV with six birdies and an eagle in the last 10 holes to win by one stroke. But perhaps Nicklaus's biggest putt was his birdie on the 16th hole at the 1975 Masters. The putt gave him the lead (a stroke ahead of Johnny Miller and Tom Weiskopf) and his fifth Green Jacket, a record that stood until 1986, when Nicklaus bagged number six.

Nicklaus's constant experimentation shouldn't be confused with a lack of confidence. The Golden Bear certainly trusted his ability. Finding his "stroke du jour" was an exercise in perfection. Moreover, it was a search for anything that could possibly give him an edge over his opponents. For the most part, Nicklaus came up aces.

Putting Tactics During Competition

Foursomes and match play are popular formats the world over. Both add a special dynamic to the game that stroke play simply doesn't provide. There are plenty of nuances to winning at match play, alternate shot, and four-man better-ball competitions, especially where putting is concerned. Here are a few ways to give you or your team an edge on the putting green.

Use Your Partner's Ball As a Backstop

In team competition, it's okay to hit another ball with your own on the putting green without incurring a penalty. So, if you have a tricky downhill putt, and your partner's ball lies behind the hole, use it as a backstop in the event you play past the hole. You can use your opponent's ball, too, but he will likely mark it if he thinks its position will give you an advantage.

Allow Your Partner to Putt Out

Your partner is away. He strokes the putt and it comes up short on the line you intend to putt along. Instead of asking him to mark the ball, allow him to putt out. Watching your partner's second putt should give you plenty of information about what yours will do.

The same advice holds true if, for example, you're putting for birdie, and your partner, who's putting for par, is inside your ball on the line of your putt. Again, instead of having him to mark the ball, ask your partner to finish out to provide you with valuable information concerning the break and speed.

Always Expect the Worst

One of the fundamental truths of match play is that you should always expect your opponent to make his putt—even from the most unlikely distances. If you tell yourself that your opponent will make the putt, you'll start in motion the thought process needed to make yours. Plus, you'll be better able to deal with the obvious pressure, having already accepted that he holes out.

A good example of this occurred at the 1999 Ryder Cup. Remember Justin Leonard's miraculous bomb on the 17th hole during Sunday's individual matches? Even after Leonard's miracle putt and the revelry that ensued, his opponent Jose Maria Olazabal remained calm. He had already told himself that Leonard would make his putt. He didn't wince, groan, or cast an upturned eye toward the heavens. He simply waited for the green to clear, set up to his putt, and nearly holed it.

Concede, Concede, Concede

A time-honored trick in match play is to concede putts early in the match. In accordance with the rules, a player cannot refuse a concession. He has to pick up. By conceding easy putts early in the round, you'll keep your opponent from the experience of having to make a short putt under pressure. You'll also curtail his feel for the conditions of the green. Later in the round, when every putt starts to mean something, make him putt out. Your opponent's unfamiliarity with the pressure and the greens could cause havoc on his nerves and stroke. Remember, in match play, always look for ways to give yourself an advantage.

Rules to Help You Score

Golf is full of rules. Most of the time, golfers view the *Rules of Golf* as "score wreckers." However, if you take the time to familiarize yourself with the *Rules*, especially those that deal with putting, then you can use

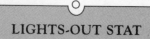

them as "score helpers." Try to think of the *Rules* as your allies. Get an understanding of the following situations, and use the *Rules* that govern them to your advantage. In the world of lights-out putting, there's no room for penalty strokes.

Ball Unfit for Play (Rule 5-3)

A ball is unfit for play if it is visibly cracked, cut, or out of round. When you approach your ball on the green, always mark and inspect it if you have reason to believe the ball may be damaged. If the ball is deemed unfit for play, you can substitute another ball without penalty. You must first announce your intentions to opponents, and allow them to inspect the ball as well. If you fail to comply with this procedure, you incur a penalty stroke or forfeit the hole during match play.

Practicing During Play of a Hole (Rule 7-2)

You're late for your tee time. You rush to the first tee, hit your drive, then hit a few putts on the practice green while the rest of your foursome tees off. Wrong! That's practicing during the play of a hole, and will cost you a two-stroke penalty or loss of hole.

You can practice your putting on the course, but only between the play of two holes, and only on the putting green you last played, on a practice green (if it's close by), or on the next tee before play begins. Often, however, local rules prohibit practice on the green in order to quicken the pace of play.

Indicating the Line of Play (Rule 8-2)

You're on the green. Your partner or caddie helps you read the line. That's perfectly okay. What your partner or caddie can't do is physically touch the green (with his foot, finger, or putter) to indicate where the break will occur or where your line of putt should go through. They can indicate these positions by pointing, but not by touching the line of putt. Otherwise, it's a two-stroke penalty or loss of hole.

You can touch the line of putt only in the following situations (Rule 16-1):

- when removing sand and loose soil on the putting surface and other loose impediments by picking them up or by brushing them aside with your hand or putter (dew is not a loose impediment)
- when addressing the ball, you can place the club in front of the ball (as long as you don't press down)
- when measuring
- when lifting the ball
- when pressing down a ball marker
- when repairing old hole plugs or ball marks

Order of Play (Rule 10)
I'm sure you know that the player farthest from the hole putts first. That's an easy rule to remember. The situation can get complicated if, for example, a player with a long putt lags his ball to tap-in range. Typically, golfers are inclined to tap these in immediately. Not so fast. You're only allowed to putt out of turn if it's allowed by your partners. If you do tap in before you've been given the green light, you must replay the stroke. Ironically, there's no penalty involved.

Repairing Ball Marks (Rule 16-1c)
Ball marks on the putting green can be repaired, even if they're on your line. Irregularities on the line, however, may not be repaired on the line of putt. Irregularities include spike marks or raised tufts of grass. Otherwise, it's a two-stroke penalty or loss of hole.

Testing the Surface (Rule 16-1d)
Be careful how you remove loose impediments. Aggressively brushing away sand or soil can sometimes be construed as testing the surface. During the play of a hole, a player can't test the surface of the putting green by rolling the ball or roughening or scraping the surface (two strokes, loss of hole).

Caddie/Partner Position (Rule 16-1f)
While making your stroke on the putting green, your caddie or partner can't stand behind you on an extension of the line of putt. They can do

so to assist your read, but once you're set to putt, have them move to the side (two strokes, loss of hole).

Ball in Motion (16-1g)

If you stroke your ball while another ball is in motion, you'll earn two penalty strokes or lose the hole (unless it was your turn to play). Be patient. Better yet, watch how your partner's or opponent's ball rolls to get a better read of the green.

Waiting for the Ball to Drop (16-2)

You stroke your putt, it rolls to the hole, then . . . unbelievable. It stops just on the edge of the hole. How long can you wait to see if it will drop? If any part of your ball overhangs the lip of the hole, you're allowed enough time to reach the hole without unreasonable delay and an additional 10 seconds to determine whether the ball is at rest. If the ball doesn't drop into the hole, it's deemed to be at rest. Careful, now. If the ball is declared to be at rest, and subsequently falls, you must add a penalty stroke to your score. Ouch!

Ball Striking the Flagstick (17-3)

The flagstick's primary function is to indicate where the hole is. Its incidental use as a backstop has been the cause of many a controversy and many changes in the flagstick rule over the years. Here are the essentials:

- If your ball is on the putting green and your ball strikes the flagstick, whether attended or unattended, the penalty is two strokes or loss of hole.
- If your ball is off the putting green, you may try to use the flagstick, while in the hole, as a backstop. There's no penalty for hitting it, as long as you didn't authorize someone to tend it.

Ball at Rest Moved (Rule 18)

A ball at rest is nothing to mess with. Through the green, if you remove any loose impediments around your ball, and the ball moves, it's a penalty. On the putting green, however, if your ball or ball marker moves during the removal of loose impediments, the ball or ball marker should be replaced. There's no penalty (unless, of course, you don't replace your ball or ball marker).

Too Much Patience

In 1990, Sam Torrance had a ball overhanging the lip during a European PGA Tour event. Torrance patiently waited for the ball to drop, as the *Rules* allow. But a videotape indicated that he waited 27 seconds! The ball eventually fell into the hole, and Torrance raised his arms in triumph, thinking he had made birdie three. Wrong. He had to card a four because he waited longer than 10 seconds.

It's a different story altogether once you address the ball. If you address your putt and the ball moves before you begin your stroke, you must replace it and penalize yourself one stroke. If you continue your stroke and putt the ball, that stroke counts, in addition to the penalty stroke. If you feel that your ball is unstable on the green, don't ground your putter. The penalty can occur only if you address the ball. Addressing a ball involves taking your stance and grounding your club. If the ball moves before you ground your putter, you must replace the ball in order to avoid the penalty.

If your ball is on the green and it's struck by another ball that was off the green, there's no penalty. Simply replace your ball. When both balls are on the putting green and a ball in motion strikes a ball at rest, the player who made the stroke must penalize himself two strokes. The owner of the ball at rest must replace his ball without penalty.

In four-ball match play, there's no penalty if you strike another ball on the putting green. In fact, many astute four-ball match players will not ask for a ball to be lifted that's behind the hole since, in essence, he or she can use it as a backstop.

Here's an odd situation, but I'm sure you've come across it before. You stroke your putt, and the ball happens to strike one of your playing partners who wasn't quite paying enough attention to what was going on. Is there a penalty? No. You can putt the ball again from its original position or play the ball as it lies.

Ball Interfering with Play (Rule 22)

According to Rule 22, you may lift your ball if you feel that it will assist another player, or have any other ball lifted if you consider that the ball might interfere with your stroke or assist another player. In stroke play, a player required to lift his ball may play first rather than lift.

Etiquette

In my opinion, a golfer isn't truly a golfer, and a lights-out putter isn't truly a lights-out putter, until he knows, comprehends, and practices good etiquette. Golf isn't a trash-talking, bad-mouthing sport. It's based on sportsmanship. This doesn't mean you shouldn't strive to win. I want you to win, but in a way that allows you to be comfortable about how you carry yourself—in your eyes and in the eyes of your opponents—while doing so.

That said, all golfers should familiarize themselves with the unwritten codes of gamesmanship. These rules of courtesy extend from tee to green, and from the moment you exit your car till the moment you leave the 19th hole. The following are the codes of etiquette I find the most important where putting is concerned:

Keep Up the Pace of Play

Many golfers believe that keeping up the pace of play is the number-one priority in terms of etiquette. Often, this forces golfers to rush their putts. If you manage your time wisely, there should be no reason why you shouldn't read your putt, perform your preputt routine, and make your stroke within a reasonable amount of time. The following are some tips to speed up play on the greens:

- If your ball is the first one to reach the green, you should be the first to read your putt.
- Start observing the speed, slope, and grain well before it's your turn to putt.
- When it's your turn to play, make sure you've already analyzed your putt.
- Be consistent; take the same amount of time on every putt regardless of its length or value (too many players overanalyze their first putt and rush their second putt if they happen to miss).
- Hole out putts that are less than 12 inches (remember to get permission from your partners).
- Practice your preputt routine before you put it into play (it should be rehearsed well before you take it to the course).

Never Walk Across a Line of Putt

This mandates that you pay attention and know where your partners' balls lie and the general line they'll take to the hole. When walking on the green, try to walk behind your playing partners' balls. If you must walk through a line of putt, be sure to step over it. Also, be sure not to tread too close to the hole: spike marks near the cup exert the greatest influence on a putt, because there the ball will typically be rolling its slowest.

Wait Your Turn

If your partners are struggling to get on the green, and you're already on the dance floor, wait for the group to convene on the putting surface. Don't attempt to putt unless your group has agreed to "ready golf" in an effort to speed up play. Not only is this in violation of the *Rules*, but it also sends a message that you don't care about your partner, his game, or the match itself. It's selfish.

Tend the Flagstick

Caddies are a luxury for most golfers. We have to help each other out. Although the *Rules* state that you don't have to tend a flagstick (even if someone asks you to do so), be courteous and do it anyway. It will speed up play and label you a good guy or gal, which is more important than being a labeled a good or bad golfer in the long run.

Be Quiet!

Everyone knows that putting is a very demanding process. It requires skill and concentration, a focus that can easily be destroyed by useless chatter, whistling, or the rattling of clubs. Give your partners the courtesy of quiet on the putting green. I'm sure you'd want the same from them.

Repair Your Ball Marks

As a general rule, repair your ball mark and two others every time you're on the green. Ultimately, this will come back to benefit you. As the saying goes, "The lie you save my be your own." Also, once your group finishes the hole, tap down any spike marks you can see, especially those around the hole. If everyone performed this altruistic task, we'd all have better greens to putt on.

To correctly repair a ball mark, stick your repair tool around the perimeter of the indentation, starting at the rear, and gently pull the

Flagstick Foibles

Has this ever happened to you? You're tending the flag, your opponent's ball comes racing at the cup, you lift the flag, and . . . oops! The cup liner comes halfway out of the hole. What do you do? It's a horrible situation, for both the putter and for the person tending the flag. The best advice is, especially if the player putting is your opponent, not to yank the cup out of the hole. Instead, leave the liner halfway out and get a good laugh at your opponent's expense. If the cup is stationary when the ball hits it, the player who struck the putt must mark his ball on the side of the hole and tap in from there without penalty, to you or to your opponent. If the cup liner is moving when the ball strikes it, the player is allowed to replay the stroke, again without penalty. To avoid this embarrassing situation, always loosen the flagstick and angle it slightly away from the player before he putts.

Here's another flagstick folly. You're tending the flag, realize the putt is moving too fast, so, out of the goodness of your heart, you purposely leave the flagstick in. Being nice hurts: that's a penalty stroke for you. If you fail to lift the flagstick because you simply weren't paying attention, or the flagstick wouldn't come out, your poor opponent incurs a penalty stroke (while you may incur a black eye, depending on your opponent). If you purposely leave the flagstick in in an attempt to get him to incur a penalty, then shame on you. You're disqualified!

compacted turf toward the center of the mark. Then take your putter and tap down the raised turf until it's once again level. Never insert your repair tool in the center of the mark or lift the turf directly upward. Remember, you can repair ball marks before and after you putt without penalty.

Afterword

Now that you've finished reading *Lights-Out Putting*, you should realize that putting is a game within the game, a distinctive component of golf that must be studied and mastered before you can achieve any true level of success. If you want to score your best, you must devote as much practice time with the putter as you do with your longer clubs.

By now you should also understand that great putters such as Ben Crenshaw, Brad Faxon, and Loren Roberts weren't born great—they learned to be great. By combining correct practice techniques with the power of positive thinking they became lights-out putters. Remember, your mind—what you think and believe—is every bit as important as a great stroke.

Once you've made the choice to believe you will be a lights-out putter, the three basic fundamentals of consistently good putting—eyes over the ball, arms hanging directly under the shoulders, and lower body balancing the weight of the upper body—become fun and easy.

The next step is to take your new attitude and mechanically sound stroke to the golf course, where you'll quickly learn that a lights-out putter is a match for any golfer. You'll lower your handicap and start winning those $5 Nassau bets. Sounds like fun, right? What are you waiting for? Go putt the lights out!

APPENDIX

The Winner's Circle

Winning Putter Models on the
1999 Professional Tours
(according to manufacturer's reports)

PGA TOUR

TOURNAMENT	WINNER	PUTTER	TOTAL PUTTS (RANK)
Mercedes Championships	David Duval	Scotty Cameron by Titleist Newport Pro Platinum	113 (1)
Sony Open	Jeff Sluman	Scotty Cameron by Titleist Newport	NA
Bob Hope Chrysler Classic	David Duval	Scotty Cameron by Titleist Newport Pro Platinum	NA
Phoenix Open	Rocco Mediate	Scotty Cameron by Titleist Big Sur	108 (4T)
AT&T Pebble Beach National Pro-Am	Payne Stewart	SeeMore Putter	83 (5) (3 rounds)
Buick Invitational	Tiger Woods	Scotty Cameron by Titleist Newport Teryllium	109 (1T)
Nissan Open	Ernie Els	Ping Anser	106 (7T)
WGC Andersen Consulting Match Play Championship	Jeff Maggert	Ping Anser	NA
Tucson Open	Gabriel Hjertstedt	Ping Zing 2	116 (57T)
Doral-Ryder Open	Steve Elkington	Ping Anser	111 (17T)

Honda Classic	Vijay Singh	Scotty Cameron by Titleist Pro Platinum	111 (15T)
Bay Hill Invitational	Tim Herron	Ping Anser 2	109 (7T)
The Players Championship	David Duval	Scotty Cameron by Titleist Newport Pro Platinum	107 (27T)
BellSouth Classic	David Duval	Scotty Cameron by Titleist Newport Pro Platinum	116 (23T)
Masters Tournament	Jose Maria Olazabal	Kevin Burns 9304	109 (7T)
MCI Classic	Glen Day	Odyssey Dual Force 380	106 (21T)
Greater Greensboro Open	Jesper Parnevik	Bettinardi putter	99 (2T)
Shell Houston Open	Stuart Appelby	Scotty Cameron by Titleist Sante Fe	106 (4T)
Compaq Classic	Carlos Franco	Odyssey Tri-Force 2	107 (11T)
GTE Byron Nelson Classic	Loren Roberts	Cobra Greg Norman	113 (13T)
MasterCard Colonial	Olin Browne	Titleist Bulls Eye	115 (43T)
Kemper Open	Rich Beem	Odyssey Tri-Force 2	109 (1T)
Memorial Tournament	Tiger Woods	Scotty Cameron by Titleist prototype	109 (10T)
FedEx St. Jude Classic	Ted Tryba	Leading Edge Short-E	115 (54T)
U.S. Open Championship	Payne Stewart	SeeMore putter	111 (8T)
Buick Classic	Duffy Waldorf	Scotty Cameron by Titleist Santa Fe Two	104 (1)
Motorola Western Open	Tiger Woods	Scotty Cameron by Titleist Pro Platinum prototype	116 (33T)
Greater Milwaukee Open	Carlos Franco	Odyssey Tri-Force 2	113 (14T)
British Open Championship	Paul Lawrie	Odyssey Tri-Force 1	112 (13T)
John Deere Classic	J. L. Lewis	SeeMore putter	111 (20T)

Cannon Greater Hartford Open	Brent Geiberger	Scotty Cameron by Titleist Coronado Two	102 (1)
Buick Open	Tom Pernice, Jr.	Ping Zing 5BZ Nickel	105 (2)
PGA Championship	Tiger Woods	Scotty Cameron by Titleist Pro Platinum prototype	115 (28)
Sprint International	David Toms	Scotty Cameron by Titleist prototype	NA
WGC NEC Invitational	Tiger Woods	Scotty Cameron by Titleist Pro Platinum prototype	117 (26T)
Reno-Tahoe Open	Notah Begay	Titleist Bulls Eye	109 (3T)
Air Canada Championship	Mike Weir	Scotty Cameron by Titleist Newport	107 (2)
Bell Canadian Open	Hal Sutton	Scotty Cameron by Titleist Newport	103 (1T)
B.C. Open	Brad Faxon	Scotty Cameron by Titleist prototype	107 (1T)
Westin Texas Open	Duffy Waldorf	Scotty Cameron by Titleist Santa Fe Two	111 (11T)
Buick Challenge	David Toms	Scotty Cameron by Titleist prototype	110 (T11)
Michelob Championship at Kingsmill	Notah Begay	Titleist Bulls Eye	106 (4T)
Las Vegas Invitational	Jim Furyk	Scotty Cameron by Titleist prototype	142 (2T) (5 rounds)
National Car Rental Golf Classic	Tiger Woods	Scotty Cameron by Titleist Pro Platinum prototype	118 (29T)
The Tour Championship	Tiger Woods	Scotty Cameron by Titleist Pro Platinum prototype	125 (22T)
Southern Farm Bureau Classic	Brian Henninger	Scotty Cameron by Titleist prototype	75 (2T) (3 rounds)
WGC American Express Championship	Tiger Woods	Scotty Cameron by Titleist Pro Platinum prototype	116 (23T)

SENIOR PGA TOUR

TOURNAMENT	WINNER	PUTTER	TOTAL PUTTS (RANK)
MasterCard Championship	John Jacobs	Never Compromise Z|I Alpha	NA
Royal Caribbean Classic	Bruce Fleisher	Never Compromise Z|I Gamma	90 (57T)
American Express Invitational	Bruce Fleisher	Never Compromise Z|I Alpha	82 (2)
GTE Classic	Larry Nelson	Dogleg Right Hog	88 (27T)
ACE Group Classic	Allen Doyle	Scotty Cameron by Titleist Newport Two	85 (7T)
Toshiba Senior Classic	Gary McCord	Taylor Made Nubbins B7	84 (6T)
Emerald Coast Classic	Bob Duval	Scotty Cameron by Titleist Newport Pro Platinum	85 (11T)
The Tradition	Graham Marsh	Odyssey Dual Force 662	52 (5T) (2 rounds)
PGA Seniors' Championship	Allen Doyle	Scotty Cameron by Titleist Newport Two	105 (1T) (4 rounds)
The Home Depot Invitational	Bruce Fleisher	Never Compromise Z|I Alpha	84 (21T)
Bruno's Memorial Classic	Larry Nelson	Dogleg Right Hog	86 (14T)
Nationwide Championship	Hale Irwin	Never Compromise Z|I Beta	84 (17T)
Las Vegas Senior Classic	Vincente Fernandez	Never Compromise Z|I Alpha	118 (12T) (4 rounds)
Bell Atlantic Classic	Tom Jenkins	Odyssey Dual Force Rossie II	89 (29T)
Boone Valley Classic	Hale Irwin	Odyssey Dual Force 660	89 (15T)
Cadillac NFL Golf Classic	Allen Doyle	Scotty Cameron by Titleist Newport Two	86 (13T)
BellSouth Senior Classic	Bruce Fleisher	Odyssey Dual Force 330	87 (27T)
Southwestern Bell Dominion	John Mahaffey	Odyssey Dual Force 224	91 (60T)

Senior Players Championship	Hale Irwin	Never Compromise Z|I Beta	106 (1) (4 rounds)
State Farm Senior Classic	Christy O'Connor	Never Compromise Z|I Gamma	82 (1T)
U.S. Senior Open Championship	Dave Eichelberger	Never Compromise Z|I Delta 2	111 (3) (4 rounds)
Ameritech Senior Open	Hale Irwin	Never Compromise Z|I Beta	83 (11T)
Coldwell Banker Burnet Classic	Hale Irwin	Never Compromise Z|I Beta	84 (8T)
Utah Showdown	Dave Eichelberger	Never Compromise Z|I Delta 2	87 (31T)
Lightpath Long Island Classic	Bruce Fleisher	Odyssey Dual Force Rossie II	88 (6T)
Foremost Insurance Championship	Christy O'Connor	Never Compromise Z|I Gamma	77 (1)
BankBoston Classic	Tom McGinnis	Never Compromise Z|I Gamma	78 (1)
AT&T Canada Senior Open Championship	Jim Ahern	Odyssey TriForce 3	113 (9T) (4 rounds)
TD Waterhouse Championship	Allen Doyle	Scotty Cameron by Titleist Newport Two	81 (1)
Comfort Classic	Gil Morgan	Dandy Professional putter	85 (11T)
Bank One Championship	Tom Watson	Odyssey Dual Force 990	79 (3T)
Kroger Senior Classic	Gil Morgan	Dandy Professional putter	79 (6T)
Vantage Championship	Fred Gibson	Odyssey Dual Force 554	80 (4)
The Transamerica	Bruce Fleisher	Odyssey Dual Force 664	83 (9T)
Raley's Gold Rush Classic	David Graham	Bettinardi putter	82 (5T)
EMC² Kaanapali Classic	Bruce Fleisher	Scotty Cameron by Titleist Napa	88 (6T)
Pacific Bell Senior Classic	Joe Inman	Never Compromise Z|I Kappa	83 (3T)
Ingersoll-Rand Senior Tour Championship	Gary McCord	Taylor Made Nubbins B7	113 (13T) (4 rounds)

LPGA TOUR

TOURNAMENT	WINNER	PUTTER	TOTAL PUTTS (RANK)
HealthSouth Inaugural	Kelly Robbins	Ram Sportsman Wizard	90 (49T) (3 rounds)
Naples LPGA Memorial	Meg Mallon	Never Compromise Z|I Alpha	NA
The Office Depot	Karrie Webb	Scotty Cameron by Titleist Del Mar Three Pro Platinum	116 (51T)
Valley of the Stars Championship	Catrin Nilsmark	Prairie Pathfinder	80 (2) (3 rounds)
Hawaiian Ladies Open	Alison Nicholas	Never Compromise Z|I Alpha	85 (3T) (3 rounds)
Australian Ladies Masters	Karrie Webb	Scotty Cameron by Titleist Del Mar Three Pro Platinum	109 (1)
Welch's/Circle K Championship	Juli Inkster	Never Compromise Z|I Alpha	115 (18T)
Standard Register Ping	Karrie Webb	Scotty Cameron by Titleist Del Mar Three Pro Platinum	115 (25T)
Nabisco Dinah Shore	Dottie Pepper	Ping Anser 2	104 (1)
Longs Drugs Challenge	Juli Inkster	Never Compromise Z|I Alpha	129 (53T)
Chick-fil-A Charity Championship	Rachel Hetherington	Odyssey TriForce 2	88 (21T) (3 rounds)
City of Hope Myrtle Beach Classic	Rachel Hetherington	Odyssey TriForce 2	57 (20T) (2 rounds)
Titleholders	Karrie Webb	Scotty Cameron by Titleist Del Mar Three Pro Platinum	119 (34T)
Sara Lee Classic	Meg Mallon	Never Compromise Z|I Alpha	82 (6T) (3 rounds)
The Philips Invitational	Akiko Fukushima	Odyssey Dual Force 330	119 (9T)
LPGA Corning Classic	Kelli Kuehne	Never Compromise Z|I Alpha	109 (1)

U.S. Women's Open	Juli Inkster	Never Compromise Z|I Alpha	111 (4T)
Rochester Invitational	Karrie Webb	Scotty Cameron by Titleist Del Mar Three Pro Platinum	117 (28T)
ShopRite LPGA Classic	Se Ri Pak	Never Compromise Z|I Kappa	80 (2) (3 rounds)
McDonald's LPGA Championship	Juli Inkster	Never Compromise Z|I Alpha	106 (1)
Jamie Farr Kroger Classic	Se Ri Pak	Never Compromise Z|I Kappa	117 (19T)
Michelob Light Classic	Annika Sorenstam	Odyssey Dual Force Rossie II	120 (32T)
JAL Big Apple Classic	Sherri Steinhauer	Ping B60	120 (49T)
Giant Eagle LPGA Classic	Jackie Gallagher-Smith	Never Compromise Z|I Alpha	86 (13T) (3 rounds)
du Maurier Classic	Karrie Webb	Scotty Cameron by Titleist Del Mar Three Pro Platinum	124 (41T)
LPGA area Web.Com Challenge	Mardi Lunn	Never Compromise Z|I Alpha	117 (25T)
Women's British Open	Sherri Steinhauer	Ping B60	NA
Firstar LPGA Classic	Rosie Jones	Odyssey Dual Force Rossie IIL	91 (32T) (3 rounds)
Oldsmobile Classic	Dottie Pepper	Ping Anser 2	111 (2T)
State Farm Rail Classic	Mi Hyun Kim	Never Compromise Z|I Beta	81 (1) (3 rounds)
Samsung World Championship	Se Ri Pak	Never Compromise Z|I Kappa	123 (13T)
SAFECO Classic	Maria Hjorth	Odyssey TriForce 2	119 (22T)
Safeway Championship	Juli Inkster	Never Compromise Z|I Alpha	83 (1T)
New Albany Golf Classic	Annika Sorenstam	Odyssey Dual Force Rossie II	105 (2)
First Union Betsy King Classic	Mi Hyun Kim	Never Compromise Z|I Beta	119 (17T)

AFLAC Tournament of Champions	Akiko Fukushima	Odyssey Dual Force 330	115 (13T)
Mizuno Classic	Maria Hjorth	Odyssey TriForce 2	NA
PageNet LPGA Tour Championship	Se Ri Pak	Scotty Cameron by Titleist Pro Platinum Del Mar Three	119 5(T)

Index